# Feminist Spirituality
# and
# the Feminine Divine

## *An Annotated Bibliography*

### Anne Carson

The Crossing Press ✳ Trumansburg, NY
*The Crossing Press Feminist Series*

Copyright © 1986 by Anne Carson
Cover and book design by David Price
Typesetting by Davis Graphic Services, Lansing, NY

Printed in the U.S.A.

**Library of Congress Cataloging in Publication Data**

Carson, Anne, 1950-
    Feminine spirituality and the feminine divine.

    (The Crossing Press feminist series)
    1. Women and religion–Abstracts.    2. Femininity of
God–Abstracts. I. Title. II. Series.
BL458. C39  1986  016.291'088042          86-4192
ISBN 0-89594-200-3

## ACKNOWLEDGEMENTS

I wish to express my gratitude to all the women and men who have made the Goddess live and to those who have helped in the present work, especially my husband David Price, who as anthropologist, editor, and companion provided encouragement, suggestions, and technical assistance; my friend, supporter, and co-conspirator Meredith Shedd; my editor, Kate Dunn; and my spiritual companions on this journey, Lakshmi and Sarasvati.

Ithaca, N.Y.
18 Ruis 9985
(28 December 1985)

# INTRODUCTION

"There is something wonderful happening. One could
call it a reclamation of something lost or forgotten,
certainly something distorted or suppressed. It comes
by many names: Moon Goddess or Divine Mother, the
feminine consciousness and yin spirit. It is the half of
divine consciousness omitted in traditional worship of
the Father God. SHE is reemerging today as the result
of the inner work of a growing number of women
artists who while in search of themselves amid
confusion of masculine and feminine roles in their own
time came upon a larger vision for all time—a mystical
feminine revelation."

Louise Calio,
"The Rebirth of the Goddess"

For over ten years women have been celebrating their womanhood
in ways not possible in organized Western religion. Whether alone or
in communities, in living rooms or on farmland, women are participating in a spiritual movement that has sprouted, branched, and is
now reaching full flower across America and in many other countries.
We have begun honoring menstruation and menopause as joyful,
wondrous events; we are sharing stories of a women's culture; we are
writing poetry, singing songs, creating artwork and theater that
reweave the threads of feminine experience.

The women's movement has challenged us to look anew at the role of
the feminine principle in history, society, and religious thought. It has
given us the courage to think for ourselves, to conduct our own research,
to write our own texts, to create our own mythology. And it has led to
the development of a feminist theology—or rather, *thealogy,* a study of
the Divine as Goddess rather than God. This thealogy has ripened into
a powerful philosophy that finds expression in many scholarly
disciplines, creative arts, and woman-centered political activities.

Feminist spirituality had its origin, some fifteen years ago, in scholarly research. With the start of the women's liberation movement, feminist researchers began to challenge the received wisdom about sex roles and male-female relations which had been handed down by male historians, psychologists, and other social scientists. As women anthropologists went to do fieldwork among tribal peoples, they found that in many societies women exercised a greater influence and authority than had been previously reported by male anthropologists, who spoke only to male informants. The simplest hunter-gatherer societies, as it turns out, are not patriarchal but egalitarian, with men and women sharing power, and with some religious rituals and sacred knowledge reserved for women alone. In other words, the domination of politics and religion by men is not always and everywhere inevitable, nor must we accept that it has always been so. Profound questions about the origins of male domination arose: if female authority was honored in some contemporary "primitive" societies, what was the world like thousands of years ago when we were all hunter-gatherers? If patriarchy has not always been with us, how and why did it come about? This questioning became part of the social criticism of the sixties and seventies, when political activists challenged many traditional assumptions about social roles, including the relationships between men and women, women and religion, and religion and society.

Radical feminists were familiar with Marxist analysis of the evolution of society, particularly with Friedrich Engels' *Origin of the Family, Private Property, and the State,* which, in positing a primordial matriarchate, adapted nineteenth-century social theory to Marxist thought. In 1974 Evelyn Reed brought a Marxist analysis of sex roles to the feminist movement with *Woman's Evolution.* Leftist social criticism also enabled women to recognize that religion in large part not only supports existing social structures but is in fact created in the image of society.

Feminists soon learned that religious organizations, like other bastions of male power, were not eager to support a radical redefinition of the secular or spiritual role of women. Instead of becoming allies with feminists against social injustice, church and temple displayed a dedication to the perpetuation of women's oppression. The Catholic policies most difficult for Americans to accept—opposition to birth control, abortion, divorce, homosexuality, marriage for priests, and female ordination—are all issues concerned with women and sexuality. The ordination of the first female Conservative rabbi was called "a sad day for Judaism." And the largely Protestant New Right has actively lobbied against the Equal Rights Amendment and affirmative action, while supporting legislation that curtails women's rights.

Everywhere in the nineteen-sixties and seventies one could see religions led by men, serving societies led by men. Yet when women looked at prehistoric and ancient cultures, everywhere was the image of the Great Goddess. In Egypt, Crete, Mesopotamia, and throughout the Stone Age ancient woman seemed to have had a sacredness grounded in her physical self which had been denigrated and suppressed for thousands of years under male domination.

In 1971 Elizabeth Gould Davis published *The First Sex*, in which this line of thinking was taken a step further: Davis declared that before the rise of what is commonly called Western Civilization, women's position in society was not merely equal to that of men, but in fact was supreme. Subsequently, she said, woman-centered civilization was violently overthrown by the male-centered forces of patriarchy. Davis was not the first writer to interpret women's history in this light, nor can her work be taken uncritically, but in presenting the first comprehensive description of what a matriarchal/gynocentric/matrifocal society might (or did) look like, she made a vitally important contribution to feminist thought. She attributed to this—in the deepest sense—mythical society the characteristics of peacefulness, harmony with nature, creativity, communalism, and vegetarianism—values that radical feminists had already begun to view as intimately connected with feminism. For the first time a matriarchal era appeared to be based on historical fact, not just political theory. Women began saying to each other, "We know what a male-dominated society is like. We know how women are portrayed in religions directed by men. What would society be like if it were dominated by feminine values? What about a religion in which God is female? Was there ever such a woman-centered society? Was it Çatal Hüyük? Was it Minoan Crete?"

Other currents also contributed to the movement. Women in the Neo-Pagan community, such as Morgan McFarland and Starhawk, began pointing out that a woman-centered religion already existed in the form of Goddess-centered witchcraft. Present-day witches regard the Craft as a traditional folk religion whose antecedent is pre-Christian paganism, an interpretation first publicly propounded in the 1920's by British historian Margaret Murray. Because the Goddess, as Mother Earth, is supreme in this tradition, many feminists consider witchcraft to be a true women's religion.

At the same time, feminist scholars who had been researching the history of women began to perceive in the great witch-hunts of the late mediaeval and early modern period an incredible outpouring of hatred for women. The actual number of women who died in the massacres has long been disputed, but even the most cursory glance at the historical evidence makes it plain that a great many women lost their lives at the hands of the male authorities of Church and State simply because of their sex. Manuals for witch-hunters declared quite baldly that *all* women should be suspected of witchcraft, and witch-finders bragged about the number of women they had convicted. Modern feminists quickly recognized the connection between witchcraft and oppression by men. Women who conduct their lives by their own rules, who do not accept a self-effacing, "feminine" role, have always been called witches. Even today, "old witch" is an epithet hurled at the woman who is pushy, bossy, or solitary—the crackpot, the Lesbian, the childless spinster. Feminists have reclaimed the image of the witch as the outrageous, assertive woman who lives outside the strictures of society and, most importantly, beyond male control. Like the Amazon, the Lesbian, and the Virgin Goddess, the Witch is One-in-Herself.

To the dismay of some traditional witches, and the alarm of some members of the feminist movement, in the mid-seventies many women began reclaiming witchcraft as a religion of, by, and for women. Today Feminist Wicca is one of the many faces of women's spirituality, just as it is but one branch of contemporary Neo-Paganism. To practitioners, the Craft and its use of magic are considered to be a woman's way of seeing: the epitome of the non-rational (not anti-rational), intuitive, relational mode of thought. Because the Craft itself is a decentralized religion, each witch must create her own sacred space, tools, and liturgy, drawing upon traditional models. Thus the practice of feminist witchcraft requires self-reliance and creativity, enhancing the self-awareness of the woman who is coming to know her own strengths and powers. Thousands of women have come to the Craft, as others have come to the Goddess, through feminism; and some witches have found feminism through their religion.

Some women, less interested in witchcraft, have been delving into the study of the Goddess as She has existed in non-European cultures and have been exploring spiritual traditions such as the shamanism of Native Americans and other peoples whose worldview is more compatible with feminist values than those of traditional religion or the New Left. Interest in ecology, parapsychology, divination, and altered states of consciousness—common features of Goddess religion—had been prevalent in the U.S. since the 1960's. And with the growth of the men's liberation and human potential movements, the importance of the Feminine in psychology and myth began to be appreciated anew. All these approaches to spirituality were fused into the feminist vision.

Some feminists have been skeptical about the Goddess movement, and some have been concerned that it will divert women from real-life issues such as adequate day-care or economic parity and into a cul-de-sac of mysticism and fantasy. Feminist spirituality and the quest for ancient matriarchies have been compared to the Ghost Dance movement that appeared among the Oglala Sioux in the 1890's, or to cargo cults in the modern Pacific—the sort of feverish messianic movement so often found among people who are oppressed and alienated.

It is true that religion may in some contexts divert people from awareness of oppression, yet religion also serves to describe social and cosmic relationships, one's history and one's place in the world—and what could be more important than redefining current patterns of power? It may also be argued that spirituality sustains women by providing the image of a better society. And in this case the world to come is one that we can work to build and can hope to see in our own lifetime.

As researchers have found over the last twenty years, the area of women's studies covers all aspects of human history and present experience. No field of study is more interdisciplinary. Much the same can be said for women's spirituality. Each book can lead the reader to three or four others, which suggest still others, in a vast tree of knowledge. In order to give this bibliography a measure of coherence, to define a point of focus if not a clear boundary around the field, let me attempt to make clear how I am using the term "feminist spirituality."

First and foremost, feminist spirituality is a religious system that insists upon the power, value, and dignity—sometimes even the superiority—of women. In some circles it is exclusively female-oriented (Dianic), in others, more inclusive. The deity is female, spoken of as the Great Mother, the Great Goddess, and thought of as either a single entity, a polytheistic many-persons-in-one Goddess, or as a symbolic Great Presence, Prime Mover of the Universe, Spark of Creation. Among North American and European women, the veneration of the ancient goddesses of Europe and the Near East has been revived, but, reflecting feminism's roots in the civil rights movement, women's spirituality has also been very receptive to non-European traditions, in particular those of Native Americans. Thus women who have a particular affinity for, say, shamanism, Buddhism, or Celtic mythology, are able to explore these traditions and shape them according to their feminist and spiritual interests. And as our lives change we may need to honor different aspects of the Goddess—at different times we might wish to visit with Kuan Yin, or to come to terms with Athena.

This polytheistic, inclusive, and holistic aspect is one of the most important qualities of feminist spirituality. Adherents vehemently reject the idea that there is One Truth and one correct path to it. Women know all too well that such an exclusivist philosophy has been responsible for more deaths in the past two thousand years than any disease or war. Rather, spiritual feminists tend to believe that there are many truths, and that the correct path is that which is correct for the seeker. Of course, the movement is not without its controversies, but because there is no single acknowledged spiritual leader or founder, nor any single corpus of sacred texts to argue over, there is little danger of schism or heresy. In a real sense, we *are* the heresy.

Spiritual feminists believe that in woman's biological rhythms and creative force are mirrored the rhythms of the Earth and the Universe; that the Goddess or the Divine is immanent within us, here in this world, and not "out there" somewhere; that the wellsprings of the

Divine Within can be called upon for spiritual and creative uses; that physical and spiritual well-being depend on maintaining harmony with nature and the seasons. Indeed, our very survival as a species demands it.

Many women also believe (or would like to believe) in a Golden Age that lasted until the Middle Bronze Age, about 5000 years ago, in which women ruled or at least held great social and religious power; when we were free, had control over our bodies and could heal them, and lived in harmony with the cosmos. This Golden Age, it is said, was overthrown in Europe and the Mediterranean area by patriarchal Indo-European nomads who killed the priestesses, destroyed the temples of the Goddess, enslaved women, and set up the rule of their father-sky god, the emblem of male domination over women and nature. There is certainly evidence for much of the Indo-Europeans' destructive activity in the Eastern Mediterranean, although little attention has yet been paid to detecting a similar sequence of events in the Americas and Asia.

Most feminists—spiritual and otherwise—believe that the Golden Age of Woman is a myth. Let it be a myth then—for the Greek word *mythos* originally meant "story," and the myth of the Golden Age and its ending is a story women tell each other. Whether the Golden Age of Matriarchy ever existed in history is not important: what is important is that the myth exists *now*, that there is a story being passed from woman to woman, from mother to daughter, of a time in which we were strong and free and could see ourselves in the Divine, when we lived in dignity and in peace. Few people take Genesis literally, but that does not make *Paradise Lost* a mere piece of fantasy. So it is with our myth of power and greatness for women. This myth has caused thousands of women around the world to actively work at building a women's culture. And *that* is real.

This bibliography is intended to serve two groups: researchers who are investigating the concept of the Goddess and the effect that male-centered religion has on women's lives and psyches, and members of the women's community who wish to become aware of the wealth of material available on the Goddess in Her many guises, how women are interacting with Her, feminist thealogy in particular, and the feminist worldview in general.

In 1974 *WomanSpirit* appeared, the first magazine devoted to feminist spirituality. Within five years there had been a veritable explosion of literature on woman-centered religion. Practical manuals and theoretical texts were published by mainstream publishers as well as by women's presses, and feminist magazines devoted entire issues to the subject. But many books have been published by small presses and can be found only in bookstores that serve the women's community. Such books are seldom reviewed in magazines with a wide circulation. The difficulty of locating these books, as well as the fact that new books and articles come out faster than they can be read, makes it quite an undertaking to bring to the reader's attention this recent outpouring of women's writing, not to mention all the titles that have been published in the past.

I have tried to include works that describe woman-centered religion, many of which were written long before the modern women's movement, as well as works of an explicitly feminist nature. Not all titles covering ancient or modern witchcraft or the role of women *in* religion are relevant, but I have selected the ones that give the most information on the concept of the Divine as feminine, and works that particularly address the relationship between women and witchcraft. I have also made a strenuous effort to include a wide selection of the books and articles that have emanated from within the feminist spirituality movement, beginning in the early 1970's.

Women's spirituality is concerned with women and with spirituality, but not all works on religion or spirituality fall into this category simply by virtue of having a female author. Woman plus spirituality does not necessarily equal women's spirituality. Womanspirit, as feminist spirituality is sometimes called, touches the fields of history, religion, mythology and folklore, anthropology and archaeology, psychology, witchcraft and occult sciences, New Age studies, parapsychology, lesbian-feminism, health, literature, and the arts. Most of the bibliographies that have appeared so far, usually as appendices to books, have focused on only one or two of these areas in support of the texts in which they appear. For example, the bibliography in Starhawk's *The Spiral Dance* concentrates on witchcraft, the Goddess, and New Age psychology. The fine bibliography by Charlene Spretnak in *The Politics of Women's Spirituality* contains works on women's studies, books about the Goddess and witchcraft, and political and ecological works, such as Rachel Carson's *Silent Spring* and Helen Caldicott's *Nuclear Madness*, which are not specifically about women or spirituality, but which independently support the feminist worldview that everything in the universe is inextricably connected. In the interest of space, Spretnak chose not to include works on the Goddess of a traditional, non-feminist nature, or "the many well-argued feminist books that urge reforms within patriarchal religion." I, on the other hand, have decided to include works that fall into both these categories. Naturally, not all works that *do* deal with the topic of women and religion would be of interest to feminists. There are many recent Christian "inspirational" books, for instance, that ignore or are even hostile to feminism.

Nor can I possibly include all that has been written on the figure that serves as the Divine Feminine within Christianity, namely the Virgin Mary. Nevertheless, I have felt that it *is* important to list some philosophical works written from within the Christian or Jewish communities that have a specifically feminist approach. Despite the fact that exasperation with sexism has compelled many thousands of women to leave their churches and synagogues in the past twenty years, there are still women who prefer to remain within, or at least have a nodding acquaintance with, their original spiritual communities while retaining their feminism.

This has been especially important for Jewish women, many of whom feel that they cannot allow themselves to abandon their heritage, however inhospitable Judaism may be to the full religious participation of women. Jewish women who re-feminize Judaism by rewriting the ancient ceremonies and texts believe that to abandon Judaism for Neo-Pagan Goddess worship, despite Judaism's own debt to the Goddess, is simply to assume yet another aspect of Gentile life.

In a similar vein, many feminists choose to remain within the Church because they find Christ's teachings powerful enough to withstand any subsequent sexist theology. Theologians such as Rosemary Ruether, Elisabeth Schüssler Fiorenza, and Carol Ochs are now exploring traditional Christian and Biblical themes from a woman-centered perspective, seeking a God who need not be rejected in the pursuit of true liberation for all. Christian feminists yearn to see a reflection of the Divine in themselves just as much as women who have utterly rejected patriarchal religious institutions, and they too need to know about recent writings on religion and sexism. I wish to address the needs of both these groups by presenting works that give new ways of looking at old religions, and works that seek to create new myths, new patterns of social and spiritual interaction.

To aid researchers I have included some items in foreign languages that have not been translated into English, as such works have not previously appeared in bibliographies of women's spirituality. The German women's movement in particular has recently produced a number of works on the Goddess and the matriarchal mythos. There are also titles in French, Spanish, Portuguese, Italian, Danish, Dutch, and Japanese, which indicates the worldwide extent of interest in the Goddess.

Like Spretnak, I have listed a few titles that are neither products of nor reflections on this spiritual movement, but which should be of more than passing interest to students of Goddess religion. Some are works of a spiritual nature that do not explicitly deal with women, and others are nonreligious works about women that have been enthusiastically taken up by feminists as reflective of our worldview. One example is *The Kin of Ata Are Waiting for You,* by Dorothy Bryant, first published in 1972 as *The Comforter.* A visionary novel about a quasi-tribal spiritual community, Bryant's story has been claimed by the women's spirituality movement because its description of this community and its ideals furnishes an image of what our community might be like if it had a permanent home. The attitude of the book is feminist, but there is no Goddess or in fact any other deity mentioned in it. I include it because of the significant influence it has had on feminist thealogy. Other examples in this category are Shakti Gawain's meditation manual, *Creative Visualization,* and Jane Roberts' *The Nature of Personal Reality.* These books have been adopted by many daughters of the Goddess as handbooks and philosophical guides, and as such have in effect become texts of women's spirituality, moving beyond their authors' original audience. Just as the student of mediaeval philosophy must eventually turn to Aristotle and Plotinus, so these ancillary works must be included as contributions to feminist spiritual thought and practice.

As for works on witchcraft, I have had to be very selective in this area, including only those works that directly relate to woman's role as witch and those that have been most supportive of the theory of witchcraft's pagan origins, since it is this pre-patriarchal aspect that attracts and inspires feminist witches. As the 1980's progress there seems to be less of an interest in witchcraft per se among feminists, at least in terms of ritual practice, as we begin to leave behind one traditional structure in order to create our own visions and philosophies. In any case, most of what has been published on witchcraft over the years is at best not relevant to our study, for most mainstream authors either focus on the witch-hunts as a bizarre but isolated chapter in European history, or else assume that witchcraft is primarily the practice of black magic as a means to gain control over others, ignoring any religious or woman-centered aspects. This is also true of the sister disciplines of the occult, including the Tarot and astrology, which women now employ as paths to self-knowledge rather than mere fortune-telling devices, so only those occult texts that are feminist-oriented or emphasize the feminine principle are included.

For more general works on witchcraft and the occult I recommend J. Gordon Melton's *Magic, Witchcraft, and Paganism in the United States: a Bibliography* (see entry 438, below) which includes a large section on background material for the study of witchcraft. This book is also useful for locating material on the magical and religious traditions of women of color, for example works on Vodun, Santeria, and Huna, the native religion of Hawaii. For primary works on European witchcraft, there is *Witchcraft: Catalogue of the Witchcraft Collection in Cornell University Library* (entry 135), which describes the largest collection on European witchcraft in this country. Should anyone, for instance, wish to determine just how many women were accused, convicted, and executed as witches during the great witch-hunts of the 15th-17th centuries, this collection of rare books and manuscripts would be invaluable.

Most of the books and articles listed here should be available at large libraries. If they are not in your area, they can be obtained on interlibrary loan through your town or county library, often for free or for a low fee. For the beginning researcher Susan E. Searing's *Introduction to Library Research in Women's Studies* (Boulder, CO: Westview Press, 1985) would be very helpful. Searing presents the basics of using a library—how to formulate a reference question, how to utilize the card catalogue and interlibrary loan—and gives an introduction to computerized reference services. She also lists and annotates subject guides, indexes, and bibliographies in many areas of research (e.g. psychology, religion, lesbian studies).

To summarize, this bibliography includes: works produced by the women's spirituality movement or inspired by it; pre-feminist works on the worship of the Goddess around the world; some journal articles on the Goddess that contribute to women's understanding of Her history and which are not for the scholar alone; major works on the mythic importance of the Feminine; works on witchcraft that stress the role of women, the Goddess, or pre-Christian religious practices; occult books with a feminist orientation; works from outside the women's spirituality or witchcraft communities that significantly contribute to our thealogy; some works on the concept of prehistoric matriarchy that reflect the mythic aspect as well as the purely historical; material on the Amazons (who are part of our mythology); theological works emanating from a traditional religious background which address the issue of the Feminine Divine; and works that create a female-centered religious environment within or without organized religion.

*Not* included are: most scholarly archaeological and historical articles on various goddesses, as they are of little interest to the general reader (although I have listed such works if they discuss women's relation to Goddess worship, the feminine principle, or contribute in an illuminating way to thealogy); most works on the position of women *in* male-centered religions (for the interested reader there are listed instead a number of general bibliographies that cover the topic of woman and religion); witchcraft and occult books that do not have a Goddess or feminist orientation; most basic texts of feminist philosophy; most fiction, especially sword-and-sorcery novels, of which there are so many nowadays; and individual poems.

Also not included are music tapes and records, for which the reader is directed to the Ladyslipper Catalogue, Box 3130, Durham, NC 27705. Ladyslipper is a collective of women who market all kinds of sound recordings by women, including many albums inspired by feminist spirituality. In the bibliography I do list lectures available on cassette, however.

To make this list useful to both the researcher and the general reader, entries are arranged under the author's surname, or forename if there is no surname. Collected works and anthologies are generally under the name of the editor rather than under title. I have preferred American editions of books first published abroad and English editions of books originally written in other languages; I have noted whether books are available in paperback, and whether they were first written as university dissertations (sometimes they are easier to obtain in this form); and I have included the date of original issue if the work is not contemporary. The titles of foreign language works are translated into English. Journal and newspaper articles are given as follows. "For our Mother who art in heaven," by Sandra Adickes, which appeared in the March 9, 1978 issue of *Win,* volume 14, number 9, pages 7-9, is cited as:

Adickes, Sandra. "For our Mother who art in Heaven," *Win,* 14(9):7-9, Mar. 9, 1970.

The opinions represented in the books, articles, and periodicals listed are many and varied. The authors are professors, students, psychotherapists, writers, poets, musicians, artists, reporters, herbalists, and just plain folks. It is all too easy to dismiss an author's work because he assumes that Christianity must be superior to "primitive" religion, or because she does not write in conformity with academic standards—turning away guests because they violate the reader's intellectual dress code. But no one exists in a vacuum; everyone ultimately belongs to a country, a time, a social class, a turn of mind.

I am sure that there are items I have overlooked, and some readers may miss their favorite titles. But I hope that many more will find in the titles I have brought together a deeper understanding of the universal presence of the Goddess.

# BIBLIOGRAPHY

1. Abbey, Lynn. *The black flame.* New York: Ace, 1982. 376 p.
2. ———. *Daughter of the Bright Moon.* New York: Ace, 1980. 410 p.

   A number of women writers are now using the literary genre of fantasy fiction to create images of powerful, free women. This and the preceding work are sword-and-sorcery stories about Rifkind, a nomadic priestess-warrior who is dedicated to the Bright Moon Goddess but also must learn to serve the Dark Moon; two entertaining novels that raise some intriguing ethical questions about the use of magical power.

3. Ackerman, Phyllis. *The first goddesses.* New York: Iranian Institute, 1940. 16 p.

   A brief study of Mesopotamian goddesses.

4. Adickes, Sandra. "For our Mother who art in heaven," *Win,* 14(9):7-9, Mar. 9, 1978.

   The author discusses the importance religion has had in her life, her realization of the religious oppression of women, and the relationship between spirituality and political activism.

5. Adler, Margot. *Drawing down the moon: witches, druids, Goddess-worshippers and other pagans in America today.* New York: Viking Press, 1979; Boston: Beacon Press, 1981. 455 p.

   Indispensable study of feminist and traditional Neo-Pagans. Adler is a reporter for National Public Radio who is also a priestess in the Gardnerian tradition of witchcraft, i.e. the tradition founded by Gerald Gardner. She spent many months in the 1970's traveling around the U.S. and England speaking with Neo-Pagans and feminist witches of many different traditions, maintaining a clear-eyed view despite her own personal involvement with the Goddess. Many of the people she interviewed talk candidly about their lives and beliefs, and provide frank and moving expositions of the spiritual philosophy of the Craft. This book is both informative and enlightening, and is a must for anyone investigating the revival of witchcraft and Goddess religion. Included are addresses of contact groups and periodicals.

6. ———. *Women, witches, and worship* [cassette]. Deland, FL: Everett/Edwards, 1978.

7. Aeschylus. *Eumenides*: a translation with commentary by Hugh Lloyd Jones. Englewood Cliffs, NJ: Prentice-Hall, 1970. 79 p.

In the third part of Aeschylus' trilogy on the Electra-Orestes myth, the trial of Orestes for the murder of his mother Clytemnestra hinges on the question: is matricide a worse crime than the murder of a husband? Apollo declares that the mother is merely the receptor of the father's seed, establishing a charter for patrilineal descent and father-rule, and heralding the eclipse of matriarchy.

8. Agrawala, Prithivi Kumar. *The glorification of the Great Goddess*. Varanasi: All-India Kashiraj Trust, 1963. 257 p.

A translation of a sacred text from the *Puranas,* the "Devimahatmya" from the *Markandeyapurana.*

9. ———. *Goddess Vinayaki, the female Ganesa.* Varanasi: Prithivi Prakashan, 1978. 44 p.

Ganesa is the popular Hindu elephant-headed god who is the representative of good fortune.

10. ———. *Goddesses in ancient India.* Atlantic Highlands, NJ: Humanities Press, 1982; based on the author's PhD thesis, Banaras Hindu University, 1971. 145 p.

Covers the Pre-Aryan and Vedic periods (contemporaneous with the European Neolithic and Bronze Ages). The author compares the Indian experience with that of Europe and the Near East. Includes many illustrations and an index of goddess names.

11. Alexiou, Stylianos. *Minoan civilization.* 3rd rev. ed. Heraclion, Greece: Spyros Alexiou, 1974? 144 p.

A general history and description of ancient Crete. Contains a chapter on religion that gives a good overview of the worship of the Great Goddess, with many examples of Cretan artwork.

12. Allegra, Donna. "SalsaSoul Sisters' Kwanza celebration," *Womanews,* 1(4):3, Mar. 1980.

SalsaSoul Sisters is an organization for Third World lesbians in New York City; Kwanza is an African winter solstice holiday.

13. Allegro, John M. *The sacred mushroom and the cross: a study of the nature and origins of Christianity within the fertility cults of the ancient Near East.* Garden City, NY: Doubleday, 1970. 349 p.

A study of the use of hallucinogenic drugs in the mystery religions, including the Mysteries of Demeter at Eleusis. Allegro's work is not woman-oriented, but he does provide a considerable amount of information on the cultic practices of the Mysteries.

14. Allen, Max. *The birth symbol in traditional women's art from Eurasia and the Western Pacific.* Toronto: Museum for Textiles, 1981. 88 p.

15. Allione, Tsultrim, comp. *Women of wisdom*; foreword by Chogyam Trunpa. Boston: Routledge and Kegan Paul, 1984. 282 p.
    Allione, a former Buddhist nun, has brought together the biographies of six Tibetan Buddhist yoginis (female yogis). Their stories tell of the ways they dealt with women's issues in their lives and how they achieved enlightenment. The author prefaces the work with her own story, describing the impact her faith and practice have had on her subsequent life as a laywoman.

16. Andersen, Jørgen. *The witch on the wall: medieval erotic sculpture in the British Isles.* New York: Allen & Unwin, 1978. 172 p.
    On the "sheela-na-gig" (Irish, loosely translates as "cunt woman"), a grinning female figure who speads her labia open; found on many mediaeval buildings, including churches, and generally regarded as a survival of the Goddess. Included is a catalog of her appearance on buildings of the 12th, 13th, and 14th centuries in Great Britain, Ireland, and France. Many photographs and drawings.

17. Anderson, Alan, and Raymond Gordon. "Witchcraft and the status of women: the case of England," *British Journal of Sociology*, 29(2):171–84, June 1978.
    An examination of the witch-hunts as a reaction to the rise of women's independence in the 16th and 17th centuries.

18. Anderson, Victor. *Thorns of the blood rose.* San Leandro, CA: Cora Anderson, 1970. 106 p.
    Poems, some about the Goddess. Anderson is a priest in the Faery tradition of witchcraft and was one of Starhawk's teachers.

19. Andrews, Lynn V. *Flight of the Seventh Moon: the teaching of the shields.* San Francisco: Harper & Row, 1984. 203 p.

20. ———. *Jaguar Woman and the wisdom of the butterfly tree.* San Francisco: Harper and Row, 1985. 194 p.

21. ———. *Medicine Woman.* San Francisco: Harper & Row, 1981. 204 p.
    This and the preceding two books, which have been compared to the works of Carlos Castaneda, chronicle Andrews' apprenticeship to Agnes Whistling Elk, a Cree holy woman; in the third volume Andrews also studies with a woman shaman in Guatemala. Like Castaneda's works they are personal narratives rather than documented anthropology.

**22.** *Anima: an experiential journal.* 1053 Wilson Ave., Chambersburg, PA 17201, 1974–.

A journal with a Jungian orientiation that covers all sorts of topics of interest: feminist spirituality, New Age psychology, mythology, etc. Many of the authors listed in this bibliography have published in *Anima.*

**23.** Apuleius, Lucius. *The golden ass of Apuleius*; translated by William Aldington. New York: Modern Library, 1932. 301 p. (There have been many other editions and translations, notably one by Robert Graves, published as *The Transformations of Lucius*, New York: Farrar, Straus and Giroux, 1951. 293 p.)

A Roman novel, also known as *Metamorphoses,* about a man who is changed into an ass by a witch and the misadventures that ensue until Isis releases him from the spell. This is still an entertaining story, both funny and sad. It includes one of the fullest extant descriptions of initiation into the mysteries of both Isis and Osiris.

**24.** Arabagian, Ruth Katz. "Cattle-raiding and bride stealing: the Goddess in Indo-European heroic literature," *Religion,* 14:107–142, April 1984.

In Indian and Irish epic literature dealing with these themes, the central female character is an avatar of the Goddess, representing Prosperity and Sovereignty. Arabagian analyzes how the Goddess dwindled in estimation under patriarchy with the clash between Indo-European and pre-Indo-European peoples. She also devotes some comparative attention to Native American and Pacific cultures.

**25.** *Arcana Mundi: magic and the occult in the Greco-Roman worlds; a collection of ancient texts.* Edited, introduced and translated by Georg Luck. Baltimore: The Johns Hopkins University Press, 1985. 395 p.

Excerpts from Greek and Roman descriptions of divination, magic, astrology and alchemy as practiced by the priestesses at Delphi and ancient witches and magicians.

**26.** Argüelles, Miriam and José. *The feminine: spacious as the sky.* Boulder: Shambhala, 1977. 152 p.

A mystical, allusive discourse on the feminine principle that draws upon Jungian psychology and Tantric Buddhism.

**27.** Aron, Albert W. *Traces of matriarchy in Germanic herolore.* Madison: University of Wisconsin, 1920. 77 p.

**28.** Arthur, Rose Horman. *The wisdom goddess: feminine motifs in eight Nag Hammadi documents.* Lanham, MD: University Press of America, 1984. 238 p.

On the Goddess as Wisdom (Sophia) in Gnostic texts.

**29.** Aryan, K. C. *The little goddesses (matrikas).* New Delhi: Rekha Prakashan, 1980. 74 p.

On the relationship between the Vedic-Tantric mother-goddesses, the letters of the Sanskrit alphabet, and mantras.

**30.** Ashe, Geoffrey. *The Virgin.* London: Routledge and Kegan Paul, 1976. 261 p.

A fascinating study of the Virgin Mary; gives a reconstructed biography and explicitly connects her to her pre-Christian antecedents. Also provides some interesting information on the Collyridians, an early Christian sect that worshipped Mary outright as a goddess.

**31.** Asherah, and Allan Greenfield. *The Al-Asherah philosophy of ecstatic dance: the new belly dance book.* Tampa, FL: Hermetic Educational Institute, 197?

Belly dancing is probably the last place one would expect to find the Goddess, corrupted as the art has become to a sexist entertainment for men. Yet the dance was originally a woman's rite, a ritual honoring the Goddess in the Near East that was taught by mothers to their daughters for centuries. For this reason some feminists and mystics have begun learning belly dancing as a means to approach the ancient ways of women.

**32.** Auel, Jean M. *The clan of the cave bear.* New York: Crown, 1980; New York, Bantam, 1981. 495 p.

**33.** ———. *The valley of horses.* New York: Crown, 1982; New York: Bantam, 1982. 502 p.

This and the preceding work are best-selling novels in Auel's "Earth's Children" series, about a Cro-Magnon woman raised by Neanderthals and her solitary quest to find other Cro-Magnons. Auel has done a great deal of research into Paleolithic, Goddess-centered culture. She names the Great Goddess Donii, which may be a close approximation to the name of the eponymous goddess of the Danube, Don, and Dnieper Rivers, Devonshire, and Denmark.

**34.** Avalon, Arthur [Sir John Woodroffe]. *Hymns to the Goddess and Hymn to Kali.* Wilmot, WI: Lotus Light Publications 1981; first edition published 1953. 335 p.

Translation of Sanskrit hymns to various Indian Goddesse including Aditi, Durga, Chandi, Devi.

**35.** ———. *The Serpent Power: being the Sat-cakra-nirupana a¡ Paduka-pancaka, two works on Laya-yoga;* translated fr( the Sanskrit, with introduction and commentary by Artl Avalon. New York: Dover, 1974; reprint of the 7th editi Madras: Ganesh, 1964. 529 p.

On Kundalini as Shakti ("female power") and as Mo

Goddess. In Kundalini or Laya Yoga, the divine creative energy is visualized as a coil spiraling up the spine, and it is identified with creative feminine energy. This is a very detailed manual, full of yogic terminology, with a translation of two Tantric texts. (This reprint has omitted the Sanskrit text which is appended to the Indian editions.)

36. Bacchiega, Mario. *Dio padre o dea madre? [God the Father or God the Mother?]* Florence: Libreria Editrice Fiorentina, 1976. 159 p.

On the femininity of God.

37. Bach, Eleanor, and George Climlas. *Ephemerides of the asteroids: Ceres, Juno, Pallas, Vesta, 1900–2000.* Brooklyn: Celestial Communications, 1973. 160 p.

Astrologically, the major asteroids represent different aspects of feminine qualities. Bach and some other astrologers are now including them in charts in order to build a more whole astrology.

38. Bachofen, Johann Jakob. *Myth, religion, and mother-right: selected writings;* introduction by Joseph Campbell. Princeton: Princeton University Press, 1967 (Bollingen Series, 84); first published in 1861. 309 p.

Bachofen was a nineteenth-century German armchair anthropologist who believed that, in the infancy of society, a period of matriarchy had preceded patriarchy, matriarchy being considered the most primitive, undifferentiated form of social organization. Under matriarchy there was no marriage as we know it, and it was women who held power in society, living communally and raising their children in common. He supported his theory by citing the long tradition of Amazon Queens and goddesses in ancient times. Like most historians of his day he assumed that the course of history inevitably meant progress, patriarchy and Classical civilization being indicative of a mature mentality that broke the bonds between men and nature. Early feminist theories of matriarchy were largely inspired by his ideas.

39. Baker, Aleta Blanche. *Man—and his counterpart—woman: or, the fifty gates of understanding.* Boston: n.p., 1930. 441 p.

40. ———. *She, the woman-man.* Boston: n.p., 1935. 338 p.

This and the preceding work are books of ritual magic with an early feminist orientation.

41. Baker, Mariam. *Woman as divine: tales of the Goddess.* 1991 Garfield St., Eugene, OR: Crescent Heart Press, 1982. 68 p.

Originally intended as a play, this is a collection of pieces on the Goddess in various manifestations as well as pieces on holy women of Sufism and other faiths.

**42.** Bamberger, Joan. "The myth of matriarchy: why men rule in primitive society," in *Women, culture, and society*, ed. Michelle Zimbalist Rosaldo and Louise Lamphere, Stanford University Press, 1973, p. 263-80.

Bamberger writes that if by "matriarchy" is meant actual political dominance by women, then matriarchy *is* a myth. In seeking evidence of women's influence we must look instead at other spheres of life than the strictly political.

**43.** Barash, David, and Judith Eve Lipton. *The caveman and the bomb: human nature, evolution, and nuclear war.* New York: McGraw Hill, 1985. 302 p.

Nuclear brinksmanship as Neanderthal mentality and the extreme form of male identification. The authors urge a return to women's values (matriotism), using goddess imagery and rituals.

**44.** Barstow, Anne. "The uses of archeology for women's history: James Mellaart's work on the Neolithic Goddess at Çatal Hüyük," *Feminist Studies*, 4(3):7-18, 1978.

Barstow is an archaeologist who visited with Mellaart at Çatal Hüyük in Central Turkey (ancient Anatolia) in 1965 (see item 436). She disputes the common belief that women had little power in ancient civilizations; at least this does not seem to be the case in Çatal Hüyük. Mellaart himself reasons that the lack of a palace or other evidence of central authority indicates that Çatal Hüyük was an egalitarian society—egalitarianism, not domination by women, being the demonstrated historical opposite of patriarchy. Barstow describes the features of the Goddess-centered religion and culture of Neolithic Anatolia. This article is a good introduction to the study of this civilization.

**45.** Beauvoir, Simone de. *The second sex.* New York: Knopf, 1952; New York: Vintage Books, 1974. 810 p.

The seminal work in modern feminist thought. One of Beauvoir's most important contributions is the recognition that patriarchy names woman as the Other, as that which is not "normal." This work is a classic analysis of what constitutes "masculine," "feminine," "male," "female." In her chapters on the history of women, Beauvoir shows that oppression has not always been women's lot.

**46.** Becher, Ilse. "Der Isiskult in Rom—ein Kult der Halbwelt? [The cult of Isis in Rome: a demimonde cult?]" *Zeitschrift für ägyptische Sprache und Altertumskunde*, 96:81-90, 1969/70.

Becher asserts that despite what many male Romans and modern historians have claimed, the cult of Isis was not characterized by promiscuity. The fact that Isis championed women's rights caused men to fear the consequences of women's freedom, and to translate "freedom" into "promiscuity." On the contrary, chastity was an important value for the devotees of Isis.

47. Beck, Jane C. "A traditional witch of the twentieth century," *New York Folklore Quarterly*, 30(2):101–16, 1974.
   A visit with a Black-Hispanic woman living in Philadelphia who was trained in her art by her grandmother.

48. Bednarowski, Mary Farrell. "Women in occult America," in *The occult in America: new historical perspectives*, ed. Howard Kerr and C. L. Crow, Urbana: University of Illinois Press, 1983, p. 177–95.
   A survey of women's role in the occult from 19th century spiritualism to the resurgence of feminist Goddess-worship.

49. Begg, Ean. *The cult of the Black Virgin*. Boston: Routledge and Kegan Paul, 1985. 272 p.
   There are more than 400 Black Madonnas extant in the world, yet their origin remains a mystery. Begg, a practicing Jungian analyst, traces the Black Virgin to her pre-Christian roots. He finds a stronger connection, however, with Gnostic Christianity, the Cathar heresy, and the traditions surrounding the legendary journey of Mary Magdalene to the South of France. Many of the Black Madonnas have been found in this region.

50. Bell, Marilyn J. "Feminist spirituality: bags, hags, and crones," *Resources for Feminist Research/Documentation sur la Recherche Féministe*, 11(2):223–24, July 1982.
   A thought-provoking article on aging and the figure of the Crone.

51. *The Beltane Papers*. Box 8, Clear Lake, WA 98235.
   A periodical devoted to women's spirituality, published eight times a year. Oriented toward Goddess religion and Neo-Paganism, but also includes contributions by authors from other spiritual traditions. Contains articles, poetry, art, music, book reviews, and announcements.

52. Bennett, Florence Mary [Florence Mary Bennett Anderson]. *Religious cults associated with the Amazons*. New York: AMS Press, 1967; PhD thesis, Columbia University, 1912. 79 p.
   Using Classical texts, Bennett describes the religion of the Amazons as centering on Artemis and Ares. She tends to assume that the Amazons were historical and not mythical figures.

53. Bennett, Lynn. *Dangerous wives and sacred sisters: social and symbolic roles of high-caste women in Nepal*. New York: Columbia University Press, 1973. 353 p.

Of most interest are chapters 2, 3, and 7, on "Religion," "Life Cycle Rites," and "The Goddess: Mythic Resolutions to the Problem of Women and Women's Problems," which look at the terrible and beneficent forms of the Hindu Goddess.

54. Bennetts, Leslie. "Judy Chicago: women's lives and art," *New York Times*, April 8, 1985, p. B6.

    A supportive article on the Birth Project exhibition (see item 115). Chicago discusses her commitment to portraying women as Creators.

55. Berger, Pamela C. *The Goddess obscured: transformation of the grain protectress from goddess to saint.* Boston: Beacon Press, 1985.

    Berger uses archaeology and folklore to examine the shift in expression of female power which took place in the early Middle Ages.

56. Berndt, Ronald M. *Kunapipi: a study of an Australian aboriginal religious cult.* Melbourne: F. W. Cheshire, 1951; New York: International Universities Press, 1951. 223 p.

    Kunapipi is the Aboriginal Creatrix-Goddess.

57. Berry, Patricia. "The rape of Demeter/Persephone and neurosis," *Spring: an annual of archetypal psychology and Jungian thought*, 1975, p. 186–98.

    Berry describes Demeter's behavior after the kidnapping of Persephone into the underworld (the realm of the soul) in terms of clinical depression.

58. Bhattacharyya, Narendra Nath. *The Indian mother goddess.* 2nd ed. Columbia, MO: South Asia Books, 1977. 319 p.

    Discusses seemingly every goddess ever mentioned in any of the Hindu scriptures and folk tradition, touching on fertility cults, matriarchy, evidence for goddess-worship in the Neolithic Indus Valley civilizations, Indian matrifocal and matrilineal societies, and the Mother Goddess in contemporary religions. The author is well-read in the current Goddess literature.

59. Biaggi De Blasys, Cristina. *Megalithic sculptures that symbolize the Great Goddess.* D.Ed. thesis, New York University, 1983. 3 vols. (689 p.)

    The author studied megalithic monuments in Malta and Scotland which reveal the pre-eminence of the Great Goddess in the Paleolithic and Neolithic Ages and show Her replacement in the Bronze Age by male-dominated polytheism. For her doctoral work the author compared motifs found among Scottish and Maltese artifacts, and also created her own Goddess sculpture in the style of the monuments she examined.

60. Biardeau, Madeleine, comp. *Autour de la déesse hindoue [On the Hindu Goddess].* Paris: Editions de l'Ecole des Hautes Etudes en Sciences Sociales, 1981. 252 p.
Essays in English and French.

61. Bjerregaard, Carl H. A. *The Great Mother: a gospel of the eternally-feminine; occult and scientific studies and experiences in the sacred and secret life.* New York: Inner-Life, 1913. 330 p.
A Theosophical text which celebrates the superiority of woman and suggests that society would be better off under a matriarchy.

62. *Black women in antiquity;* edited by Ivan Van Sertima. New Brunswick, NJ: Transaction Books, 1984. (Special issue of the *Journal of African Civilizations,* v. 6, no. 1, April 1984.) 159 p.
Contains articles by women and men on the Queens of Ethiopia and Egypt, "The Female Horuses and Great Wives of Kemet," "Egypt's Isis: the Original Black Madonna," "African Goddesses: Mothers of Civilization," "The Image of Woman in African Cave Art," and "African Warrior Queens." *The Journal of African Civilizations,* which Van Sertima edits, is dedicated to uncovering Black people's contributions to Western civilization. Anyone studying the ancient civilizations of Africa and Egypt would find each issue of interest.

63. Bleeker, C. J. *Hathor and Thoth: two key figures of the ancient Egyptian religion.* Leiden: Brill, 1973. (Studies in the History of Religions, 26) 171 p.
Hathor was an indigenous Egyptian goddess who over the millenia was depicted as cow, tree, mother goddess, sun, and sky. As Cleopatra called herself "daughter of Isis," so the Pharaoh often referred to himself as "the son of Hathor." Thoth was the ibis-headed moon god, associated with peace and the rule of law.

64. ———. "Isis as Saviour Goddess," in *The Saviour God,* ed. S. G. F. Brandon. Manchester: Manchester University Press, 1963, p. 1–7.
Isis gave her followers the promise of eternal life and in ancient times was widely regarded as a saviour, much as the Messiah was.

65. Blofeld, John. *The bodhisattva of compassion: the mystical tradition of Kuan Yin.* Boulder: Shambhala Press, 1978. 158 p.
The most comprehensive recent book on Kuan Yin. Blofeld discusses her transformation from the male Avalokita of India to her present female form and describes her iconography. He relates many lovely stories about her influence and intercession.

**66.** Bloodroot Collective. *The political palate: feminist vegetarian cooking.* Bridgeport, CT: Sanguinaria Publications, 1980. 325 p.

A fine cookbook compiled by the owners of a feminist restaurant in Bridgeport. The recipes are arranged according to the eight Sabbats in the Wheel of the Year (Late Autumn, Early Winter, etc.), beginning with Witches' New Year, Halloween. They consciously use foods that are in season. Almost every page is accompanied by a quotation from women's writing and music, and there is also an introductory essay on women and food and the need to attune ourselves to the seasons. The bibliography includes many feminist and spiritual works as well as cookbooks.

**67.** ———. *The second seasonal political palate: a feminist vegetarian cookbook.* Bridgeport, CT: Sanguinaria Publishing, 1984. 241 p.

This edition, which contains almost all new recipes, is arranged in just four seasons. There are many more introductory essays on food, feminist politics, and the lessons learned by the collective. Appended are another feminist bibliography and "A Witch Recipe for Grievers," giving Wiccan thoughts on death.

**68.** Blue Moonfire. A matriarchal zodiac. 16 Sandwell Mansions, West End Lane, London, NW6 1XL. 168 p.

Woman-centered astrology with imagery of Goddesses and mythic female figures. The planets are given the names of the appropriate Greek goddesses, e.g. Jupiter becomes Themis, Saturn becomes Rhea. While Thorsten's *God Herself* (see entry 656) may have been the first Goddess-oriented astrology book, this is a more practical and technical work for women who already have a fair knowledge of astrology and the construction of horoscopes and charts.

**69.** Bolen, Jean Shinoda. *Goddesses in Everywoman: a new psychology of women.* San Francisco: Harper and Row, 1984. 334 p.

Bolen is an Asian-American psychoanalyst who utilizes Greek mythology to illustrate the different psychological and relational patterns a woman may experience in her life. She feels that each woman tends toward one or more of the archetypes suggested by the major Greek goddesses: for example, the independent virgin goddesses Artemis, Athena, and Hestia; the "vulnerable goddesses" Hera, Demeter, and Persephone, who teach us about love; or the "alchemical goddess," typified by Aphrodite, who is able to give and receive love without sacrificing her autonomy. Bolen's intent is to help women gain insight into our own psyches by bringing an appreciation of Greek mythology and Jungian archetypal theory to a wide audience.

70. *A book of pagan rituals.* Rev. ed. New York: Weiser, 1978. 142 p.

    A Gardnerian manual and introduction to Neo-Paganism; Goddess- and nature-oriented. Gives solitary and group rituals for the Full Moon and Sabbats, chapters on herbs and healing, rituals for marriage, divorce, and initiation.

71. Bord, Janet and Colin. *Earth rites: fertility practices in pre-industrial Britain.* London, New York: Granada, 1982. 273 p.

    A general work on the survival of the Goddess and the pagan gods in folk tradition.

72. Böttcher, Helmuth. *Die grosse Mutter: Zeugunsmythen der Fruhgeschichte [The Great Mother: creation myths of early history].* Dusseldorf: Econ-Verlag, 1968. 379 p.

    From Paleolithic goddesses to Mary.

73. Bowman, Charles H. *The goddess 'Anatu in the ancient Near East.* PhD thesis, Graduate Theological Union, Berkeley, CA, 1978. 314 p.

    The author studied Anatu (Anat) as she appears in Ugaritic and Egyptian texts. Anatu was a virgin goddess of sexuality and war, associated with the god Baal as consort or sister. In Egypt she was the consort of the dark god Seth. Rameses II was devoted to her in her war goddess aspect.

74. Bradley, Marion Zimmer. *The mists of Avalon.* New York: Knopf, 1983. 876 p.

    A most impressive retelling of the story of Arthur from the point of view of Morgan le Fey, who in this version is a priestess of the pre-Christian religion of the Goddess. Set explicitly in fifth-century Celto-Roman Britain, Bradley's story details the conflict between the new Christian religion and the druids and priestesses of the Old Religion, giving many new interpretations of familiar Arthurian motifs. Despite some anachronisms, this novel is a major contribution to the body of work surrounding the Arthurian legends, and can easily take its place beside Malory and the novels of T. H. White.

75. Branston, Brian. *The lost gods of England.* 2nd ed. New York: Oxford University Press, 1974. 216 p.

    Branston discusses more gods than goddesses, but he makes the point that little is known about Anglo-Saxon goddesses because by the time the Germanic tribes reached Britain they were already a patriarchal society. However, this is still a good source for Anglo-Saxon paganism.

76. Brelich, Angelo. "Offerte e interdizioni alimentari nel culto della Magna Mater a Roma" [Offerings and food prohibitions in the cult of the Magna Mater at Rome], *Studi e Materiali di Storia della Religioni*, v. 36, 1965, p. 27-42.

77. ———. *Vesta*. Zurich: Rhein-Verlag, 1949. 120 p.
    A German translation from the original Italian. Deals with Vesta as Mother, as Virgin, and as fire-goddess; the origins of her worship, her virgin priestesses, and the significance of their chastity.

78. Briffault, Robert. *The mothers*. New York: Macmillan, 1931. 3 vols. (There are many other editions of this work, including a one-volume abridged edition: London: Allen and Unwin, 1959. 451 p.)
    A comprehensive, if now outdated, anthropological survey of matrilineal societies and the power women have exercised in primitive culture. Like Bachofen, Briffault believed that a matriarchal period preceded patriarchy. This work begins as a study of the evolution of consciousness and turns to an examination of the biological and social evolution of motherhood and the family. Of most interest are vol. 1, chapter 17, on taboos, especially taboos applied to women; chapter 19, on "The Witch and the Priestess"; chapters 20-22, on the moon and primitive religion; and vol. 2, chapter 7, on matriarchy and matrifocality in European and Asian civilizations. There is a considerable amount of data on sexual and marital customs among non-Western tribal peoples. Many feminist theorists have been influenced by Briffault's work.

79. Brindel, June Rachuy. *Ariadne: a novel of ancient Crete*. New York: St. Martin's Press, 1980. 246 p.
    A bleak story, told alternately by Ariadne and a cynical Daedalus, of the last days of the Goddess religion in Crete. Theseus is depicted as an arrogant, violent young conqueror. A unique and original version of the myth.

80. ———. *Phaedra: a novel of ancient Athens*. New York: St. Martins Press, 1985. 227 p.
    The story of the mythic heroine Phaedra, who was a child and a minor character in *Ariadne,* and her marriage to Theseus, the conquering patriarchal hero. Brindel has reworked the traditional myth into a largely original story.

81. Broner, E. M. *A weave of women*. New York: Holt, 1978; New York, Bantam, 1980; Bloomington: Indiana University Press, 1985. 296 p.
    A novel about a group of women from all walks of life, Jewish and Gentile, living on a kibbutz, who form a community that becomes a true family of women. The sisterly

feeling among them is most powerful, as they perform rituals that exorcise the demons of oppression from within them.

82. Brown, Cheever M. *God as mother: a feminine theology in India; an historical and theological study of the Brahmavaivarta Purana.* Hartford, Vt.: Claude Stark & Co., 1974. 264 p.

A scholarly work originally presented as the author's thesis at Harvard University.

83. Brubaker, Richard L. *The ambivalent mistress: a study of South Indian village goddesses and their religious meaning.* PhD thesis, University of Chicago, 1978. 403 p.

84. Brumfield, Allaire Chandor. *The Attic mysteries of Demeter and their relationship to the agricultural year.* New York: Arno Press, 1981. 227 p. (PhD thesis, University of Pennsylvania, 1976, written under the name of Chandor.)

Describes in detail nine seasonal festivals of Demeter and Persephone, including the Mysteries and the Thesmophoria. The author pays special attention to the all-woman character of some of the rites. An excellent source of information on woman-centered worship of Demeter.

85. Bruns, J. Edgar. *God as woman, woman as God.* New York: Paulist Press, 1973. 89 p.

The femininity of God from a Catholic perspective.

86. Bryant, Dorothy. *The kin of Ata are waiting for you.* Berkeley: Moon Books, 1976; originally published as *The comforter*, 1972. 220 p.

A wonderful novel about a mysterious spiritual community with a Christlike heroine. The story is told by a man who is successful as a writer but abominable to women; he gets into a fiery car crash and wakes up having been somehow transported to a faraway island, where he slowly learns spiritual wisdom through trusting his dreams. Although this novel is not actually about the Goddess or feminist spirituality, its vivid description of a community whose ideals are compatible with women's spirituality has been quite influential among feminists.

87. Buckland, Raymond. *Witchcraft from the inside.* 2nd ed. St. Paul: Llewellyn Publications, 1975. 144 p.

A good introduction to the Craft, its pagan origins, and its connection with the Goddess. Includes a chapter on Vodun as African witchcraft. Buckland is a Gardnerian witch.

88. Budapest, Z [Zsuzsanna]. "The death of a witch," *Sister,* 10(3):7, June 1979.

89. ———. "Feminist Wicca folding," *Sister,* 10(2):8, Apr. 1979.

The Feminist Wicca was the name of Z's occult shop and bookstore.

**90.** ———. "From the tripod" [newspaper column], *Sister,* 9(1):10, Feb. 1978; 9(3):12, June 1978; 9(6):7, Dec. 1978.

**91.** ———. *The Holy Book of Women's Mysteries.* Oakland: Susan B. Anthony Coven No. 1, 1979/80. 2 vols. [Originally published in a shorter version as *The feminist book of lights and shadows,* Venice, CA: Feminist Wicca, 1976.]

Z is a feminist witch who learned many of her skills from her mother in Hungary. In 1971 she began to orient her witchcraft toward the Goddess; in 1975 she was arrested for reading Tarot cards, and at her trial defended fortune-telling as part of women's ancient religion. That she admitted to being a witch was controversial; but her insistence that witchcraft and feminism were inextricably linked was nothing less than revolutionary. Witchcraft and feminism have never been the same since. Her *Holy Book* was the first specifically feminist ritual manual and has been enormously influential. In it she writes of Goddess-lore, rituals, spells, herbs, and candles with humor and imagination. The second volume contains original ceremonies for happy and sad life events such as birthdays, menarche, menopause, abortion/miscarriage, loss of reproductive organs, and rape, none of which are provided for in the Judeo-Christian tradition.

**92.** ———. "Our own religion: Wicca sisterhood," *Sister,* 5(10):3, Feb.1975.

Z has been a strong advocate of Goddess-religion as being for women only.

**93.** ———. "Politics of women's religions," *Bread and Roses,* 2(3):26, 28–29, Autumn 1980.

**94.** ———. *The rise of the Fates.* Los Angeles: Susan B. Anthony Coven No. 1, 1976. 91 p.

A play about the resurgence of women's religion.

**95.** ———. *Selene: the most famous bull-leaper on earth.* Oakland: Diana Press, 1976. 52 p.

A children's book set in Minoan Crete. Selene is a little girl who wants to participate in ritual bull-leaping and receives help from the goddess Diana.

**96.** ———. "Witch is to woman as womb is to birth," *Quest,* 2(1):50–56, Summer 1975.

On the natural connections between women and witchcraft.

**97.** *The burden of Isis: being the laments of Isis and Nephthys,* translated from the Egyptian, with an introduction by James T. Dennis. New York: Dutton, 1910. 59 p.

From an ancient Egyptian poem. The relationship between Isis and her sister Nephthys has been said to have Sapphic overtones.

**98.** Burland, Cottie Arthur. *Echoes of magic: a study of seasonal festivals through the ages.* London: P. Davies, 1972; Totowa, NJ: Rowman and Littlefield, 1972. 234 p.

On nature festivals in Britain and their sexual components. Includes a calendar of saints' days and other festivals. The author finds the magical atmosphere of the ancient rites to be far superior to what passes for ritual in twentieth-century Western civilization.

**99.** Cahill, Suzanne E. *The image of the goddess Hsi Wang Mu in medieval Chinese literature.* PhD thesis, University of California at Berkeley, 1982. 2 vols.

Hsi Wang Mu, the Queen Mother of the West, is the chief goddess of Taoism. Cahill examines the character of Hsi Wang Mu from her earliest appearance to the time of the T'ang dynasty, concentrating on her image in Chinese poetry.

**100.** Caldecott, Moyra. *The lily and the bull: a novel set in Minoan Crete.* New York: Hill and Wang, 1979. 177 p.

A story in which a group of priestesses try to usurp the Queen's power by promoting bull-worship over the religion of the Goddess of the Lilies.

**101.** Calio, Louise. "A rebirth of the Goddess in contemporary women poets of the spirit," *Studia Mystica,* 7(1):50–59, Spring 1984.

A poet examines women's spirituality as reflected in the works of Plath, Sexton, and Shange.

**102.** Cameron, Anne. *Daughters of Copper Woman.* Vancouver, BC: Press Gang Publishers, 1981. 150 p.

Stories of mythic and contemporary women from the Nootka people of Canada's west coast. The first half of the book relates stories of the matriarchal ancestress Copper Woman and her descendants; the remaining chapters are tales of Nootka women's history and ritual life, as told to a young Nootka woman by her grandmother. Cameron writes that these stories were told to her by the members of a secret matriarchal society. However much she may have modified them, the voices of the Nootka women come forth with a stunning clarity.

**103.** Campbell, Joseph. *The masks of God,* vol. 1: *Primitive mythology.* New York: Viking Press, 1959. 504 p.

Classic work on pre-patriarchal religion, centering on the role of myth and ritual in tribal society. Campbell also describes the place of the Mother Goddess among contemporary tribal peoples, Paleolithic cave-dwellers, and the early Near Eastern civilizations. This is an excellent source of information on what are presumed to be the religious practices and beliefs of prehistoric people, with many comparisons made to non-Western cultures.

104. Capra, Fritjof. *The Tao of physics.* Boulder: Shambhala Publications, 1975. 330 p.

     The Womanspirit/New Age worldview sees the universe as an interconnected whole, rather than a collection of discrete and separate parts. There is no distinction between humanity, nature, and the underlying cosmic forces. In this respect feminist spirituality is more similar to ancient Eastern religions than to Western traditions of philosophy and science. Capra, himself a physicist, explains that the holistic worldview of Taoism, Buddhism, Hinduism, and Zen is sustained by the discoveries of modern physics, which suggest that everything in the cosmos does, indeed, flow together.

105. Carol, Chris. *Amazon baby: songs for women.* Portland, OR: the author, 1977. 31 p.

106. ———. *Rainbow warrior woman: songs to celebrate life on earth, songs for lovers, songs for keeping the peace, songs for women.* Sunny Valley, OR: New Woman Press, 1983. 30 p.

107. ———. *Silver wheel: songs of womanspirit, for seasons and circles.* Sunny Valley, OR: New Woman Press, 1979-80. 2 v.

     Volume 1 was issued as: *Silver Wheel: Thrice Thirteen Songs*; volume 2 is entitled: *Lunar Calendar and Song Cycle for Women's Chorus.* Chris Carol is the foremost songwriter of feminist spirituality.

108. Cassuto, Umberto, ed. *The goddess Anath: Canaanite epics of the patriarchal age*; translated from the Hebrew by Israel Abraham. Jerusalem: Magnes Press, Hebrew University, 1951. 194 p.

     Canaanite texts on the Goddess, with an English translation (from the Hebrew), and commentary.

109. Cavin, Susan. "Lesbians have natural rhythm," *Majority Report*, 5(14):15, 20, Nov. 15-29, 1975.

     On lesbians and jazz music, with information on lesbians in Vodun in nineteenth-century New Orleans.

110. Chappell, Helen. *The waxing moon: a gentle guide to magick.* New York: Links Books, 1974. 214 p.

     An introduction to witchcraft and magic, illustrated by the author. She looks at the western magical tradition, herbal magic, Vodun, ritual magic, and the use of amulets and talismans.

111. Chaudhuri, Dulal. *Goddess Durga, the Great Mother.* Calcutta: Mrimol Publishers, 1984; Columbia, MO: South Asia Books, 1985. 66 p.

     Durga is one of the more popular avatars of Shiva's consort, also known as Kali, Parvati, or Chandi.

**112.** Chen, Ellen. "Nothingness and the Mother principle in early Chinese Taoism," *International Philosophical Quarterly,* 9(3):391-405, 1969.

**113.** ———. "Tao as the Great Mother and the influence of motherly love in the shaping of Chinese philosophy," *History of Religions,* 14(1):51-64, 1974.

In this and the preceding article Chen points out that in the evolution of Taoism in China, just as in the West, there seems to have been a period of matriarchy, or at least of matrifocal culture, preceding patriarchy. She identifies the all-encompassing Tao with the maternal principle.

**114.** Chew, Willa. *The Goddess faith.* Hicksville, NY: Exposition Press, 1977. 222 p.

Chew has her own brand of Goddess religion, apparently influenced by the Orphic mysteries and without much explicit feminism. An appendix contains an excellent glossary of the occult.

**115.** Chicago, Judy. *The birth project.* Garden City, NY: Doubleday, 1985. 231 p.

The chronicle of an exhibition of her designs celebrating birth, executed in needlework and weaving by women around the country. Chicago began working on images of birth and creation in 1980, basing them upon folklore and mythology and on women's actual birth experiences. Her drawings and paintings were converted into needlework panels by many other women. In the book each of the 80 designs is illustrated by the needlework and is accompanied by descriptions of the work by Chicago and the woman who actually created the textile piece.

**116.** ———. *The Dinner Party: a symbol of our heritage.* Garden City, NY: Anchor Press/Doubleday, 1979. 255 p.

Chicago designed a series of dinner plates, accompanied by needlework placemats and table settings, in commemoration of 39 (3 x 13) goddesses and historical women, ranging from the Primordial Earth Mother to Georgia O'Keefe. The china images are of incredibly powerful vulvar motifs, each relating in some way to the character of the woman or goddess it represents. The entire work traveled around the U.S. as an art exhibition. This book contains illustrations and a history of the creation of the plates, which Chicago sees as a revival of the women's art of china-painting, and brief descriptions of 999 goddesses and historical women whose names were embroidered on the tablecloth.

**117.** ———. *Embroidering our heritage: The Dinner Party needlework.* Garden City, NY: Anchor Books, 1980. 287 p.

This book covers the needlework runners created for *The Dinner Party*, tracing the socioeconomic foundation of needlework as a women's artform. It is as much a history of women and art as it is a chronicle of Chicago's exhibit.

118. ———. "Revelations of the Goddess," *Coevolution Quarterly*, no. 21, p. 54–58, Spring 1979.

A feminist creation myth, describing the creation of the universe, primordial harmony of society, and the Fall, perpetrated by men. Illustrated by Goddess images taken from *The Dinner Party* plates.

119. Choquette, Diane. *The Goddess walks among us: feminist spirituality in thought and action; a select bibliography.* Berkeley: Graduate Theological Union Library, 1981. 7 p.

A checklist of works pertaining to women and religion held at the Graduate Theological Union Library, which has been actively collecting material on women's spirituality and New Age religions.

120. Christ, Carol P. *Diving deep and surfacing: women writers on spiritual quest.* Boston: Beacon Press, 1980. 159 p.

A good introduction to the theme of women's spirituality. Christ examines spiritual expression in the works of a number of women writers, including Margaret Atwood, Doris Lessing, and Ntozake Shange, making a strong case for women's need to celebrate female experience. In most of the works under consideration the Divine is ultimately found to reside within the self.

121. ———. "The new feminist theology: a review of the literature," *Religious Studies Review*, 3(4):203–10, Oct. 1977.

In this article Christ surveys the newly emerging writing on women's spirituality and cautions that the reader must not be fooled into thinking that this social and intellectual movement is insignificant simply because, to the mainstream, male-identified academic world, some of the writing may at first seem poorly reasoned or amateurish.

122. Christ, Carol P., and Judith Plaskow, eds. *Womanspirit rising: a feminist reader in religion.* San Francisco: Harper and Row, 1979. 287 p.

A collection of essays on woman's place in traditional and post-patriarchal religion that is an excellent starting place for the new reader. Contributors include Z Budapest, Mary Daly, Naomi Goldenberg, Elaine Pagels, Starhawk, Rosemary Ruether, and others represented in this bibliography. The first group of articles lays bare the fundamental sexism of Western religion (although the female-founded religions of Shakerism,

Christian Science, and Seventh-Day Adventism are not discussed); the second section deals with the history of women in the religions of the Near East and Europe; the third is concerned with attempts to re-feminize Christianity and Judaism; and the final section describes the new paths feminism is forging in spiritual thought.

**123.** *Chrysalis: a magazine of women's culture.* Los Angeles, 1978-.
See especially no. 6, Fall 1978: contains articles by Daly, Spretnak (a good survey of the literature of women's spirituality), and Chellis Glendinning's *"Star Wars* and the Old Religion,"* in which the author interprets the war between the Empire and the Jedi rebels as a clash between patriarchal and feminist values.

**124.** *Circle Network News.* Box 9013, Madison, WI 53715, 1980-.
A quarterly newspaper of Neo-Paganism, with comprehensive coverage of many occult and pagan topics. Includes a women's spirituality column.

**125.** *Circle of Cerridwen.* 10196 152nd St., Surrey, BC, Canada V3R 6N7.
Periodical.

**126.** Clement, Carol, and Z Budapest. *1977: a year and a day calendar.* Baltimore: Diana Press, 1976. 16 p.

**127.** Cles-Reden, Sibylle von. *The realm of the Great Goddess: the story of the megalith builders.* Englewood Cliffs, NJ: Prentice-Hall, 1962. 328 p.
The author describes the Goddess-worshipping cultures that extended from the Near East to Ireland. Many wonderful photographs of megalithic monuments and statues of the Goddess.

**128.** Colegrave, Sukie. *The spirit of the valley: androgyny and Chinese thought.* London: Virago Press, 1979; published in the U.S. as: *The spirit of the valley: the masculine and feminine in the human psyche.* Los Angeles: Tarcher, 1981. 244 p.
An excellent explication of the right-brain vs. left-brain modes of thought. The author uses Taoism to show the dualism inherent in patriarchal thinking, adding that the unconscious cannot be truly appreciated without the conscious.

**129.** Collins, Sheila D. *A different heaven and earth: a feminist perspective on religion.* Valley Forge, PA: Judson Press, 1974. 253 p.
A fundamental critique of patriarchal religion.

**130.** Collum, Vera C. C. *The Tressé Iron-Age megalithic monument*

*(Sir Robert Mond's excavation): its quadruple sculptured breasts and their relation to the Mother-Goddess cosmic cult.* London: Oxford University Press, 1935. 124 p.

The first part describes a megalithic gravesite in France, which has no other ornamentation than four breasts sculptured on it; the second part describes the philosophy of ancient Goddess-religion, becoming a fascinating excursion into Pythagoreanism, Druidism, and the concept of the Word (Logos).

131. ——. *Various aspects of the male-female creative principle, with special reference to the Messenger as Word and as guide in ancient oriental religion, and in the Celtic-speaking world, and their survival in Ireland, Scotland, Britain, and Armorica.* Guernsey, Eng.: Société Guernésiaise, 1935. 168 p.

132. Columbia University. Southern Asian Institute. *Goddess in Indian art: two lists of objects exhibited 1) at Columbia University, March 3–March 7, 1980; 2) at the Brooklyn Museum, February 27–June 30, 1980.* New York: Columbia University, 1980.

An exhibition catalogue.

133. *The coming age.* Lux Madriana, 40 St. John St., Oxford, Eng.: The Madrian Society, 1976–.

A quarterly publication published by the Madrians, an English Goddess-worshipping group that comes from a different tradition than Paganism or feminism.

134. Cook, Katsi. "The women's dance: reclaiming our powers," *Indian Studies* (Ithaca, NY), 2(2):14–16, Fall 1985.

Cook, a Mohawk woman who is an editor of the magazine, describes the female-based creation myths of some Native American peoples, the important relationship between women and the moon in Native philosophy, and the power ascribed to women in traditional communities. She stresses that it is vital for women keep the old ways alive.

135. Cornell University Libraries. *Witchcraft: catalogue of the Witchcraft Collection in Cornell University Library,* ed. Martha J. Crowe; introduction by Rossell Hope Robbins; index by Jane Marsh Dieckmann. Millwood, NY: KTO Press, 1977. 644 p.

The collection consists of some 3,000 books and manuscripts, mostly primary sources from the 16th through the 18th centuries—including many original treatises on witchcraft and records of trials and prosecutions. It constitutes the largest collection on this subject in the U.S. One of the collection's strong areas is critical works by sixteenth- and seventeenth-century eyewitnesses to the witch-hunts.

**136.** *Country Women.* Albion, CA, 1972-.

Issue 10, April 1974, is devoted to women's spirituality. This issue was the genesis of *WomanSpirit* and contains several contributions by *WomanSpirit*'s editors and creators, Ruth and Jean Mountaingrove. Included are articles on various spiritual traditions, poetry, and songs.

**137.** Courtot, Martha. *Tribe.* San Francisco: Pearlchild Press, 1977. 28 p.

A collection of majestic poems told in the voices of women who live, love, celebrate, and build together.

**138.** *Covenant of the Goddess Newsletter,* c/o Alison Harlow, Box 3716, Stanford, CA 94305.

Published 13 times a year at the full moons. One of the most important Goddess and Neo-Pagan periodicals, published by a legally recognized church that is a federation of over fifty groups.

**139.** Crawford, Osbert G. S. *The eye goddess.* New York: Macmillan, 1958. 168 p.

From Egypt to Ireland, the Goddess was often artistically represented by one or two eyes. The two-eyed motif was frequently in the form of a double spiral, symbolizing the rebirth of the soul.

**140.** Craighead, Meinrad. *The Mother's songs: images of God the Mother.* New York: Paulist Press, 1985.

Paintings of God as Mother from a Catholic perspective.

**141.** Crowther, Patricia. *Lid off the cauldron: a handbook for witches.* London: Muller, 1981. 156 p.

Crowther is a British Gardnerian witch. This manual is rather male-oriented but contains some useful information on spells and divination.

**142.** Crowther, Patricia and Arnold. *The witches speak.* Introduction by Leo Martello. New York: Weiser, 1976. 145 p.

Apparently this book was actually written by Arnold Crowther and completed by his wife after his death. The Crowthers describe Wicca as a pre-Christian nature religion whose deities are the Mother Goddess and her consort the Horned God. They are extremely critical of the Christian church's bigotry toward witchcraft. The book includes a chapter by a Christian man who writes sympathetically of modern witchcraft. Attractively illustrated with drawings of the Goddess and God.

**143.** Culpepper, Emily E. "Female history: myth making," *Second Wave,* 4:14-17, 1975.

144. ———. *Philosophia in a feminist key: revolt of the symbols.*
Th.D. thesis, Harvard University, 1983. 2 vols. (578 p.)
A critique of feminist symbolizing, drawing on Daly,
Beauvoir, and philosopher Susanne K. Langer. She examines
thealogy as "gynergetic symbolizing," and discusses the
transforming power of psychic self-realization and the identification of oneself as an Amazon.

145. ———. "The spiritual movement of radical feminist consciousness," in *Understanding the new religions*, ed. Jacob Needleman and G. Baker, New York: Seabury Press, 1978, p. 220-34.
A good overview of the feminist spirituality movement.

146. Cunningham, Scott. *Earth power: techniques of natural magic.*
St. Paul: Llewellyn Publications, 1983. 153 p.
A manual of Wicca-based nature religion that concentrates
on magic practiced with the four elements—earth, air, fire,
and water—and natural entities such as wind, trees, stones,
and sea.

147. ———. *Magical herbalism: the secret craft of the wise.* St. Paul:
Llewellyn Publications, 1980. 243 p.
The magical, as opposed to healing, properties of herbs. The
author describes the Craft philosophy of magic and gives
practical advice on using herbal preparations; spells for
protection, love, etc.; directions for making incense and oils;
and folk names of plants.

148. Lady Cybele. *Witches and Halloween* [cassette]. Circle, Box
9013, Madison, WI.
A witch of the Welsh tradition, Lady Cybele discusses the
pagan origins of Halloween and the survival of ancient
customs to the present day.

149. Dahl, Katrin. *Thesmophoria: en graesk kvindefest [Thesmophoria: a Greek women's festival].* Copenhagen: Museum
Tusculanum, 1976. (Opuscula Graecolatina, no. 6) 147 p.
Describes the festival and gives a feminist analysis of its
significance for women. In Danish and Greek, with an English
summary on p. 95-101.

150. Daleen, Leitner L. B. *Tales of two women: a comparative study
of the Homeric Hymn to Demeter and the Book of Ruth.* MA
thesis, Florida State University, Tallahassee, 1984. 89 p.
Both works are famous for their depiction of bonding
between women.

151. Daly, Mary. "After the death of God the Father: women's
liberation and the transformation of Christian consciousness,"
*Commonweal*, 94:7-11, Mar. 12, 1971.
This article contains the seeds of much of Daly's radical

theology which she was to expand upon in *Beyond God the Father*. Here she explains for the first time how the Judeo-Christian tradition with its father-God legitimates male domination of women. She writes that feminist Christians will have to deal with the maleness of Christ by questioning the significance of the Incarnation, and that women must reject male-centered positions on sexuality and reproduction, the abuse of the environment, and violence as a political strategy.

152. ———. *Beyond God the Father: toward a philosophy of women's liberation.* Boston: Beacon Press, 1973. 225 p.; 2nd ed., with a new introduction, Beacon Press, 1985.

A landmark book which deftly dissects concepts that Christian theologians take for granted, e.g. the Fall, sin, self-sacrifice. Rather than worshipping a Father God as *a* being, Daly urges us to interpret God as Being itself, i.e. as a process of becoming. She prophesies that a feminist theology will forge a new morality that is not saturated with male concerns and values and will create a new image of the Divine that transcends the historic Christ.

153. ———. *The Church and the second sex: with a new feminist postchristian introduction by the author.* New York: Harper & Row, 1975 (originally published 1968). 229 p.

A critique of the Catholic Church's view of women, past and present. When she wrote this book, at the dawn of modern feminism, Daly still considered herself a Catholic and hoped to reform the Church. Within a few years, however, Daly had broken with patriarchal religion altogether; in her new introduction she describes her earlier work as a superceded historical document.

154. ———. "The church and women: an interview with Mary Daly" [conducted by L. I. Stell], *Theology Today*, 28(3): 349–54, Oct. 1971. (Originally published in *American Report*, May 14, 1971.)

Daly discusses the women's revolution as the Second Coming, whether sisterhood is different from brotherhood, and advises women to leave religious bodies that refuse to confront sexism.

155. ———. *The fire of female fury* [cassette]. Los Angeles: Pacifica Tape Library, 1980. 104 min.

A lecture given at Berkeley, March 15, 1980, on Hags, Amazons, and gynocide.

156. ———. *Gyn/Ecology: toward a metaethics of feminism.* Boston: Beacon Press, 1978. 485 p.

A stirring indictment of patriarchy's intellectual and physical war on women. In the first section Daly describes patriarchal thinking and how it is so pervasive that it is difficult to describe it without participating in it. The middle section is a descent into the depths, as Daly describes in detail the many atrocities perpetrated against women throughout history. There are separate chapters on the burning of Hindu widows, Chinese footbinding, African female genital mutilation, the European witch-hunts, and American medicine. In the final section she envisions entirely new modes of thought for women and expands her reshaping of language, giving new meaning to the expression "Revolting Hag." The uncompromising radicalism of Daly's thought has antagonized some feminists; it might be more useful to view this work as a form of guerilla theater that stimulates by shocking us.

157. ———. *The sexual caste system* [cassette]. New Haven: Paul Vieth Christian Education Service, Yale Divinity School, 197-. 60 min.

A lecture on sexism in language, religion, and society.

158. ———. "The spiritual revolution: women's liberation as theological re-education," *Andover Newton Quarterly*, 12(4):163–76, 1972 (also printed in *Notre Dame Journal of Education*, 2(4):300–12, 1972).

A powerful article, in which Daly states that feminism is a challenge to patriarchal Christianity which will transform social relationships. The entire issue of *ANQ* is devoted to religion and feminist thought.

159. ———. "The women's movement: an exodus community," *Religious Education*, 67:327–35, Sept. 1972.

The women's movement forms an exodus community by walking away from patriarchal bondage in order to found something new.

160. Dames, Michael. *The Avebury cycle.* London: Thames & Hudson, 1977. 240 p.

On the Avebury megalithic monuments and ancient Goddess religion.

161. ———. *The Silbury treasure: the Great Goddess re-discovered.* London: Thames and Hudson, 1976. 192 p.

Dames's thesis is that the great Silbury Hill barrow is dedicated to the Great Goddess, rather than being the grave of some unknown king, which is the usual interpretation given by archaeologists. He gives a fascinating picture of pre-Christian, pre-Celtic religion in Britain.

162. Damon, Betsy. "7000 year old woman," *Heresies*, 1(3):11, Fall 1977.

A description of a performance art piece. Damon has performed many other public rituals that empower the participants and reveal the presence of the Goddess in all women.

163. Davis, Elizabeth Gould. *The first sex.* New York: Putnam, 1971; Harmondsworth: Penguin, 1972. 382 p.

This book was the first comprehensive, post-feminist description of the Golden Age of Matriarchy; it gives a clear picture of the features of a matriarchal culture. Davis's work is visionary rather than scientific; it has had an enormous effect upon feminist thought. She believes that there was a high civilization predating the civilizations of Mesopotamia which was matriarchal and Goddess-oriented in character, and which she identifies with the archaeological remains uncovered at Çatal Hüyük in Central Anatolia. The book also describes the overthrow of matriarchal civilization by nomadic, patriarchal Indo-Europeans, and follows the fortunes of women up to the nineteenth century. The flaws of her arguments notwithstanding, for many women feminist spirituality began with this book.

164. Dematrakopoulos, Stephanie A. "Hestia, Goddess of the hearth: notes on an oppressed archetype," *Spring,* 1979, p. 55-76.

The author considers Hestia to be generally neglected by scholarship. She describes the goddess's place in ancient literature, her association with fire, salt and water, virginity, and the circle, and her mythic connection to Hermes.

165. ———. *Listening to our bodies: the rebirth of feminine wisdom.* Boston: Beacon Press, 1982. 199 p.

Describes how the biological facts of our lives—menstruation, birth, sexuality, aging—can reveal profound spiritual truths. Dematrakopoulos observes that a woman can achieve great wisdom through experiencing her body and attending to its interaction with time and with the world.

166. Devereux, Georges. *Femme et mythe.* Paris: Flammarion, 1982. 341 p.

Devereux uses goddesses such as Hera, Aphrodite, Athena, and Artemis in a psychoanalytic study of bisexuality and ambisexuality among Greek gods and goddesses.

167. Deveria, Théodule. *Noub, la déesse d'or des égyptiens: lecture faite dans la seance du 29 juillet 1853 [Noub, the Egyptian goddess of gold: lecture given at the meeting of July 29, 1853.* Paris, 1853. 26 p.

168. Dhal, Upendra Nath. *Goddess Laksmi: origin and development.* New Delhi: Oriental Publishers and Distributors, 1978. 229 p.

Lakshmi (Laksmi) is an important goddess of abundance and prosperity.

**169.** Dickensheid, Diane. "Women and revolutionary religion," *Womanews,* 5(1):14, Dec. 1983-Jan. 1984.
A report on a symposium on "Women, Religion, and Social Change" held at Hartford Seminary, Oct. 21-22, 1983.

**170.** Dietrich, Albrecht. *Mutter Erde: ein Versuch über Volkreligion [Mother Earth: a study of folk religion].* 3rd enlarged edition. Leipzig: B. G. Teubner, 1925. 157 p.
A study of the Goddess as Earth Mother with an emphasis on Greek religion.

**171.** Diner, Helen [Berta Eckstein-Diener]. *Mothers and Amazons: the first feminine history of culture.* Garden City, NY: Anchor Press, 1973; first published in 1929. 254 p.
Like Davis's work, this is a study of the great matriarchal culture that fell during the Bronze Age. It contains a great deal of information on Amazons and gynocentric elements in ancient religion, and has been very influential in feminist spiritual thought. Despite its informal style—no sources are given for any of the material—this sixty-year-old work holds up quite well.

**172.** Dini, Vittorio. *Il potere delle antiche madri: fecondità e culti delle acque nella cultura subalterne toscana [The power of the ancient mothers: fertility and water-cults in lower Tuscan culture].* Torino: Boringhieri, 1980. 224 p.

**173.** Dinnerstein, Dorothy. *The mermaid and the minotaur: sexual arrangements and human malaise.* New York: Harper and Row, 1977. 270 p.
Dinnerstein uses mythology to describe the bases for sex roles, showing how rigid gender distinction oppresses women and harms everyone's psyche. She is especially critical of the mother-centered tradition of childrearing, which forces sons to first rebel against the feminine and then strive to control it.

**174.** Di Prima, Diane. *Loba.* Berkeley: Wingbow Press, 1978. 190 p.
A poem cycle on the Goddess as wolf ("loba"). The poems are majestic and full of violent imagery. Di Prima shows us the Goddess in the junkie, the bag lady, the mental patient.

**175.** Donovan, Frank. *Never on a broomstick.* Harrisburg, PA: Stackpole Books, 1971; New York: Bell Publishing, 1971. 256 p.
A popular examination of witchcraft that recognises the pagan origins of Wicca and the misogynist character of the witch-hunts.

**176.** Downing, Christine. *The Goddess: mythological representations of the feminine.* New York: Crossroad, 1981. 250 p.

The feminine psyche revealed through Jungian analysis of Greek goddesses (Persephone, Ariadne, Hera, Athena, Artemis, Aphrodite, the Divine Child), with many examples drawn from Downing's life. She is especially interested in Athena as the father's daughter and in Aphrodite, who teaches us love and self-knowledge through relationships with others. Beautifully written, a wise and healing book.

177. ——. *Religious life and feminine experience.* Philadelphia: Friends General Conference, 1978. 14 p.
A lecture given at the conference.

178. Drinker, Sophie. *Music and women: the story of women in their relation to music.* New York: Coward McCann, 1948; Washington: Zenger Publications, 1977. 323 p.
Drinker describes women and music from the earliest days of recorded history to the present, with a look at many non-Western cultures. There is great emphasis on the spiritual and ritual elements in music.

179. DuBois, Page. *Centaurs and Amazons: women and the prehistory of the Great Chain of Being.* Ann Arbor: University of Michigan Press, 1982. 161 p.
The Great Chain of Being is the concept that there is a hierarchy in the cosmos: God/men/women/children/animals, etc. This is a philosophical work on the ancient Greek concept of difference and hierarchy as it began to appear in the fifth century B.C. DuBois documents some of the origins of oppositions in Western thought such as male/female, human/animal, etc., and shows how they support racism and sexism.

180. Dumais, Monique. "Voyage sur les sources: quelques discours féministes sur la nature [Voyage to the sources: some feminist discourses on nature]," *Studies in Religion/Sciences Religieuses*, Waterloo, Ont., 13(3):345–52, Summer 1984.
Dumais examines the concept of nature (the natural world and its philosophical connotations) as it relates to the position of women, drawing heavily on the thought of Mary Daly and French feminist Hèléne Cixous. Daly and Cixous reclaim the view of woman as wild, primeval, natural, and dynamic, redefining Nature as an active force of transformation, not a passive element waiting to be acted upon.

181. Dumézil, Georges. *Dèesses latines et mythes vèdiques [Latin goddesses and Vedic myths].* Brussels: Latomus, 1956; New York: Arno Press, 1978. 123 p.
Essays on four minor Roman goddesses and their parallels in Vedic mythology.

182. Durdin-Robertson, Lawrence. *Communion with the Goddess.* Huntington Castle, Clonegal, Enniscorthy, Eire: Cesara Publications, 1976-78. 5 v.

   Durdin-Robertson and his sister Olivia founded a sect of Goddess religion, the Fellowship of Isis, that is largely influenced by ritual magic.

183. ———. *The cult of the Goddess* [later issued as *The religion of the Goddess*]. Clonegal, Eire: Cesara Publications, 1975. 28 p.

184. ———. *The goddesses of Chaldea, Syria and Egypt.* Clonegal, Eire: Cesara Publications, 1975. 440 p.

   A dictionary of goddesses that gives the origins of their names, their relationships to other gods and goddesses, and some of their most important religious and mythological features.

185. ———. *The goddesses of India, Tibet, China, and Japan.* Clonegal, Eire: Cesara Publications, 1976. 532 p.

   A similar dictionary that gives many names of goddesses not found in most sources.

186. ———. *Juno Covella: a perpetual calendar of the Fellowship of Isis.* Clonegal, Eire: Cesara Publications, 1982. 454 p.

187. Dworkin, Andrea. *Woman hating.* New York: Dutton, 1974. 217 p.

   The history and philosophy of patriarchal fear and hatred of women and how this philosophy has been supported by the religious, legal, and medical establishments, resulting in countless atrocities against women throughout history. She includes a chapter on the witch-hunts as gynocide and as genocide against the remaining followers of the Old Religion.

188. Dykewoman, Elana [Elana Nachman]. *They will know me by my teeth.* c/o W.I.T. Inc., Box 745, Northampton, MA: Magaera Press, 1976. 117 p.

   Short stories and poetry with a matriarchal theme.

189. Eaton, Alfred W. *The Goddess Anat: the history of her cult, her mythology, and her iconography.* PhD thesis, Yale University, 1964. 164 p.

   Anat was a pre-patriarchal Semitic goddess (see entry 73).

190. Eaton, Evelyn. *The shaman and the medicine wheel.* Wheaton, Ill.: Theosophical Publishing House, 1982. 212 p.

   An account of the author's spiritual apprenticeship to Native Americans.

191. Eaubonne, Françoise d'. *Les femmes avant le patriarchat*

*[Women before patriarchy].* Paris: Editions Payot, 1976. 239 p.

Women in society from Paleolithic times through megalithic, Celtic, and Egyptian cultures. A good companion to Diner, Davis, and Fisher.

192. Eberz, Jakob [Otfried]. *Sophia und Logos, oder die Philosophie der Wiederherstellung [Sophia and Logos, or the philosophy of reconstruction].* Munich: Reinhardt, 1967. 615 p.

The Gnostic concept of the feminine, its antecedents, and its survival into Christianity.

193. Ecumenical Women's Center. *Woman-soul flowing: words for personal and communal reflection.* 5253 N. Kenmore Ave., Chicago 60640: Ecumenical Women's Center, 1978. 114 p.

A collection of liturgies, Bible readings, dramatic pieces, retold Creation stories, poetry, and songs for Christian feminists. There are separate sections for the four seasons and the observation and celebration of women's joys and pains. Liturgies deal with the separation between men and women, women's stewardship of the earth, hysterectomy, and many other women's issues.

194. Edelson, Mary Beth. *Mary Beth Edelson lecture* [videotape] Chico, CA: Instructional Media Center, California State University at Chico, 1978. 2 cassettes, 75 min.

A lecture with slides on the Goddess and women's spirituality.

195. ——. *Seven cycles: public rituals.* New York: A.I.R., 1980. 63 p.

Descriptions and illustrations of Edelson's rituals to the Goddess, some of which are private and many of which include audience participation. Introduction by art historian and critic Lucy Lippard.

196. Ehrenreich, Barbara, and Deirdre English. *Witches, midwives, and nurses: a history of women healers.* 2nd ed. Westbury, NY: Feminist Press, 1973. 48 p.

A history of women in medicine, from mediaeval women healers to the present. Describes how men suppressed women's healing knowledge out of jealousy of their powers.

197. Ekenvall, Asta. *Batrachians as symbols of life, death, and woman.* Göteborg, Sweden: distributed by Göteborg University Library, 1978. (Kvinnohistoriskt Arkiv, 14). 50 p.

Batrachians are toads and frogs, which have been pervasive symbols of the womb and of woman in her fertility aspect. The womb was at times believed to be a kind of frog with an independent existence. This work is accompanied by many unusual illustrations of frog-shaped goddesses from Paleolithic figures to European folk motifs.

**198.** Eliade, Mircea. *Occultism, witchcraft, and cultural fashions: essays in comparative religions.* Chicago: University of Chicago Press, 1976. 148 p.

Eliade, one of the world's foremost historians of religion, has written extensively on shamanism and primitive religion. Of greatest interest in this collection is chapter 5, p. 69–92, "Observations on European Witchcraft." Eliade is very critical of Margaret Murray's theories, but he does recognize the survival into historical times of the Dianic fertility cult in Romania and Italy. The final chapter is on sex in witchcraft, which he compares with ritual practices in Gnosticism and Tantric Buddhism.

**199.** *The Elvenstone.* 242 Brentborough-on-Broadmeade, Sheridan, OR 97378.

Quarterly newsletter for Neo-Pagan (Wiccan) women.

**200.** Emerson, Nathaniel B. *Pele and Hiiaka: a myth from Hawaii.* New York: AMS Press, 1978 (reprint of Honolulu, 1915). 250 p.

A long myth about the two sister goddesses, in English and Hawaiian, with an interpolated commentary.

**201.** Engelsman, Joan Chamberlain. *The feminine dimension of the divine.* Philadelphia: Westminster Press, 1979 (PhD thesis, Drew University, 1976). 203 p.

A thoughtful overview of the relationship between woman and the divine, the suppression of the Feminine in Christianity, and the concept of the femininity of God. Engelsman suggests balancing the masculinity of the Trinity by adding Mary as a fourth person of the godhead, or actively envisioning the Holy Spirit as feminine.

**202.** Evans, Arthur. *Witchcraft and the gay counterculture.* Boston: Fag Rag Press, 1978. 180 p.

A very interesting and outrageous book. Evans uses Margaret Murray's theories to show that lesbianism and homosexuality were an integral part of witchcraft in Europe and that gay people were among the chief targets of the witch-hunters. He points out that Joan of Arc was executed for her transvestism as much as for her supposed witchcraft.

**203.** Evans-Wentz, W. Y. *The fairy faith in Celtic countries.* N.p.: University Books, 1966 (reprint of 1915). 524 p.

A long study of the belief in fairies, with some suggestions as to its origins and many accounts by country people who have seen fairies. The author connects the belief in fairies to the survival of the Old Religion and discusses Murray's theory that the fairies were nothing less than the pre-Celtic, Neolithic inhabitants of Britain.

**204.** *Exhibition on Mother Goddess, 1981.* Simla, India: State Museum, Dept. of Languages and Culture, Himachal Pradesh, 1981. 45 p.

**205.** Fabian, Klaus-Dietrich. *Aspekte einer Entwicklungsgeschichte der römisch-lateinischen Göttin Iuno [Aspects of a developmental history of the Roman-Latin Goddess Juno].* PhD thesis, Freie Universität, Berlin, 1978. 216 p.
A scholarly study of the origin and history of the worship of Juno.

**206.** Fairfield, Gail. *Choice-centered Tarot.* 2nd ed. Box 31816, Seattle: Choice Centered Astrology and Tarot, 1982. 153 p.
A psychologically-oriented work which is becoming increasingly popular among feminists. Fairfield uses the Tarot images not as emblems of what *will* happen, but as information on what *may* happen if the questioner does not choose to alter her course of action.

**207.** Farians, Elizabeth. *Selected bibliography on woman and religion, 1965-72: articles, books, newsletters, news stories, organizations.* 5th ed. Cincinnati: the author, 1973. 30 p. (Available from the author, 6125 Webbland Place, Cincinnati, Ohio 45213.)
Items arranged chronologically, primarily dealing with women in Christianity, with some titles on Judaism. Includes articles from a wide range of publications.

**208.** ———. *Papers on feminism and religion.* 1965-79. 120 p.
Material written and/or collected by Farians, housed at the Graduate Theological Union Library, Berkeley, CA.

**209.** Farmer, Penelope. *The story of Persephone.* New York: William Morrow, 1973. 48 p.
A children's version of the myth; a good introduction for kids.

**210.** Farnell, Lewis R. "Sociological hypotheses concerning the position of women in ancient religion," *Archiv für Religionswissenschaft,* v. 7: 70-94, 1904.
Lists classical and secondary references to such features of matrifocal religion as the exclusion of men from certain rituals, the pre-eminence of the Goddess and the priestess, and cross-dressing. He denies, however, that these features prove the existence of a political matriarchy.

**211.** Farrar, Stewart. *What witches do: the modern coven revealed.* New York: Coward, McCann, 1971; rev. ed., Custer, WA: Phoenix Pub.Co., 1983. 184 p.
A thorough description of rituals, beliefs, and practices by a British witch of the tradition founded by Alex Sanders (Alexandrian).

**212.** Fellowship of Isis. *Isian News.* Huntington Castle, Clonegal, Enniscorthy, Eire.
Quarterly publication.

**213.** Fiorenza, Elisabeth Schüssler [Elisabeth Schüssler-Fiorenza]. "Feminist theology as a critical theology of liberation," *Theological Studies*, 36(4):605-26, Dec. 1975.
The entire issue of this journal is devoted to the subject of women in religion and women's role in the traditional church. The author, a Catholic theologian, criticizes the Church's historical sexism and androcentrism as well as the occasional lame attempts by the hierarchy to point to feminism within Christian doctrine (Pope Paul VI stated that the Virgin Mary was in fact a model for the liberated woman, citing her courage to question). Fiorenza then looks at the historical record of sexism and feminist values within the Christian community and suggests new myths for women, such as a redefinition of the role of Mary, and a recognition of Mary Magdalene as an apostle.

**214.** Fischer, Clare Benedicks. *Breaking through: a bibliography of women and religion.* Berkeley: Graduate Theological Union Library, 1980. 65 p.
Covers mostly Judeo-Christian religion. A review of the literature is followed by non-feminist works and feminist scholarship, listed separately.

**215.** Fischer, Clare Benedicks, and Rochelle Gatlin. *Woman: a theological perspective; bibliography and addendum.* Berkeley: Graduate Theological Union, Office of Women's Affairs, 1975. 70 p.
Most of the more than 900 entries deal with women in Christianity, but the authors have used a creative interpretation of "women and religion" and include titles on women in society, art, and psychology, arranging the entries by subject area. The intent of the bibliography was to support seminary curricula, providing students with sources for the study of women in theology.

**216.** Fisher, Elizabeth. *Woman's creation: sexual evolution and the shaping of society.* Garden City: Anchor Press, 1979; New York: McGraw-Hill Paperbacks, 1980. 484 p.
Women's position in society from Paleolithic times to the Bronze Age. Fisher believes that the oppression of women was contemporaneous with the beginnings of animal husbandry, which she sees as the oppression of nature. Describes the substitution of patriarchal for matriarchal values. This is a good updated companion to *The First Sex.*

217. Fleischer, Robert. *Artemis von Ephesos und verwandte Kult-statuen aus Anatolien und Syrien [Artemis of Ephesus and related cult statues in Anatolia and Syria].* Leiden: Brill, 1973. (Etudes preliminaires aux religions orientales dans l'Empire Romain, t. 35). 449 p.

A scholarly treatment of the depiction of Artemis throughout the Hellenistic world. Many illustrations.

218. Forfreedom, Ann *Califia, the Black Amazon Queen of California.* San Diego: Andromeda Press, 1973. (Mimeographed paper held at the Women's Center Library, 46 Pleasant Street, Cambridge, MA 02139.)

Califia was the legendary queen of an all-woman nation on an island off California, supposedly named for her. This society is said to have existed several hundred years before the arrival of the Spanish.

219. ———. *Feminist Wicce works.* Typescript, 1980. 35 p.

A collection of her works on the Goddess and witchcraft, written 1978–80. "Wicce" is the feminine form of "Wicca" in Anglo-Saxon. At the Graduate Theological Union Library, Berkeley, CA.

220. ———. "Matriarchies," *Everywoman,* 1(14):7, Feb. 5, 1971.

Description of what constitutes a matriarchal society.

221. ———. *Mythology, religion, and women's heritage.* Sacramento, CA: Sacramento City Unified School District, n.d. 80 p.

At the Graduate Theological Union Library.

222. ———, and Julie Ann, comps. *The Book of the Goddess.* Box 19241, Sacramento, CA 95819: Temple of the Goddess Within, 1980. 346 p.

A collection of essays, rituals, poetry, and artwork by many women, including Starhawk and Z Budapest. An excellent compilation.

223. Forrest, Katherine V. *Daughters of a coral dawn.* Tallahassee: Naiad Press, 1983. 226 p.

A visionary science fiction novel of a world of women who worship a Mother Goddess.

224. Fortune, Dion [Violet Mary Firth]. *Aspects of occultism.* New York: Weiser, 1978 (originally published 1962). 87 p.

Fortune was a member of the important occult society the Hermetic Order of the Golden Dawn. She wrote many books on the occult, parapsychology, and mysticism. This collection of essays includes a chapter entitled "The Worship of Isis," on women as natural priestesses. She also discusses the pagan gods, Druid circles, meditation, Christianity and reincarnation, and many other occult topics.

**225.** ——. *Moon magic: being the memoirs of a mistress of that art.* London: Aquarian Press, 1956; York Beach, ME: S. Weiser, 1981. 241 p.

Novel of a modern priestess of Isis. Effective use of a mystical atmosphere.

**226.** ——. *The sea priestess.* London, 1938; New York: S. Weiser, 1972. 316 p.

Novel about a priestess of the Goddess who transforms herself into Morgan le Fey of Arthurian legend.

**227.** Fox, Selena. *Circle guide to Wicca and Pagan resources.* Madison, WI: Circle Publications, 1979-.

An annual guide that gives names of individuals and groups for contact and addresses of bookstores, occult supply shops, and periodicals. The author is a Wiccan high priestess and one of the founders of Circle, a Neo-Pagan retreat in Wisconsin. She has been one of Neo-Paganism's most active and articulate spokespeople.

**228.** ——. "Wicca: channeling the Goddess within," *Bread and Roses*, 2(3):24–29, Autumn, 1980.

**229.** ——. "Witchcraft," *Frying Pan* (Eugene, OR), 8(3):11, Sept. 1983.

**230.** ——. "Witchcraft: a modern revival," *Frying Pan*, 8(6):14, Dec. 1983.

**231.** Fran Moira. "One part of the whole," *Off Our Backs*, 6(9):2–3, 11, Dec. 1976.

On the New York Spirituality Conference, held Halloween weekend, 1976, at Richmond College, Staten Island, N.Y. The author describes her own feelings about and relationship to women's spirituality before the conference and reports on the workshops she attended on self-defense, matriarchy, witchcraft and ritual, and politics and spirituality.

**232.** Franz, Maria Louisa von. *An introduction to the psychology of fairy tales.* 4th ed. Zurich: Spring Publications, 1978. 160 p.

A study of the anima and the female Shadow (the dark side of the psyche), by a Jungian psychoanalyst.

**233.** ——. *Problems of the feminine in fairy tales.* New York: Spring Publications, 1972. 194 p.

A intriguing study of popular as well as some lesser-known fairy tales. Franz reveals the presence of the Goddess in many familiar characters, and has some useful insights into the female psyche.

**234.** Frazer, Sir James G. *The Golden Bough: a study in magic and religion.* 3rd ed. London: Macmillan, 1911-15. 12 vols.; 1 vol. abridged edition, New York: Macmillan, 1979. 864 p.

This is a classic work on myth and primitive religion. Anyone doing research into mythology, folklore, or ancient religion should look at Frazer, even if much of his work has been superceded by now.

235. Freitas, João de. *Oxum Marê, Nossa Senhora da Conceicão [Oxum Marê, Our Lady of Conception].* Rio de Janeiro: Livraria Freitas Bastos, 1965. 304 p.

This goddess (or spirit) of the Afro-Brazilian folk religion of Umbanda is directly related to the Virgin Mary. The author gives the origins and lore of her cult and the rites and beliefs associated with it.

236. Friedrich, Paul. *The meaning of Aphrodite.* Chicago: University of Chicago Press, 1978. 243 p.

For Friedrich, an anthropologist by profession, the meaning of Aphrodite is that, alone among the major Olympian Goddesses, she was venerated both as a mother and as a sexual being. He includes a chapter on Aphrodite's most famous devotee, Sappho, describing her as the first poet in recorded history to deal with the personal.

237. Gagé, Jean. *Matronalia: essai sur les dévotions et les organisations culturelles des femmes dans l'ancienne Rome [Matronalia: essay on women's devotions and cultural organizations in ancient Rome].* Brussels: Latomus, 1963. 289 p.

The Matronalia was a women's festival held March 1 in honor of Juno Lucina, or Juno as Mother. In Rome as in other oppressive societies, religion offered women an outlet for expressions of power, creativity, and sisterhood, the Matronalia being one of the most important opportunities for Roman women. Gagé discusses the mythic and ritual aspects of the festival and its organization by the women. He also refers to the Sacred Marriage and the woman-only character of some other Roman festivals, e.g. that of Bona Dea.

238. Gage, Matilda Joslyn. *Woman, church, and state: a historical account of the status of woman through the Christian ages; with a reminiscence of the matriarchate.* New York: Arno Press, 1972 (reprint of 2nd edition, 1900); also published as: *Woman, church, and state: the original exposé of male collaboration against the female sex*; introduction by Sally Roesch Wagner, foreword by Mary Daly. Watertown, MA: Persephone Press, 1980 (reprint of 1893 edition). 554 p.

Nearly a century ago Gage had a startlingly modern analysis of the oppression of women as being grounded in and supported by Judeo-Christian religion. She also recognized that women had been persecuted as witches partly because of their special knowledge of healing and other powers.

**239.** Garcia, Jo, and Sara Maitland, eds. *Walking on the water.* London: Virago Press, 1985. 214 p.

A collection of essays by British feminists on feminism and spirituality, from Christian, Jewish, and Goddess perspectives. Included are two articles by Monica Sjöö; a story about the mediaeval mystic Dame Julian of Norwich; a painting of God as Mother by Meinrad Craighead; and many personal narratives.

**240.** Gardner, Gerald. *The meaning of witchcraft.* London: Aquarian Press, 1959. 283 p.

Gardner is considered to be the father of modern witchcraft— some would say its inventor. With the repeal of British laws against witchcraft in 1952, Gardner was free to write publicly about his participation in the Craft. Whatever the truth may be about the origins of modern Wicca, his books contain a great deal of useful information and background into European paganism. In this book he describes witchcraft in Britain, its pre-Christian antecedents, the Druids as practitioners of Celtic goddess-religion, and the Craft philosophy of magic.

**241.** ———. *Witchcraft today.* London: Rider, 1954. 192 p.

In his first book about the Craft, Gardner gives a detailed exposition of witch beliefs and practices, refuting traditional misconceptions about witchcraft, such as Black Masses and black magic. He believes that the fairies may have been Britain's Neolithic, pre-Celtic inhabitants.

**242.** Gardner, Kay. "Music and women," *Paid My Dues,* 2(1):8, Fall 1977; 2(2):26, Winter 1978.

Gardner is a musician who has done a great deal of research into ancient modes of music and the ways in which music affects the psyche and health. She has recognized that there is a difference between men's music, which tends to build up to a climax, and women's music, which often repeats its motifs cyclically. In the past decade she has produced four albums of music with a feminist sensibility: *Mooncircles, Emerging, Moods and Rituals,* and *A Rainbow Path* (see the Ladyslipper Catalogue—the address is in the introduction, p. 10).

**243.** Gates, Doris. *Two queens of heaven: Aphrodite, Demeter;* illus. by Trina Schart Hyman. New York: Viking Press, 1974; New York: Puffin Books, 1983. 94 p.

A children's book that retells the stories of Persephone and several of Aphrodite's myths.

**244.** ———. *The warrior goddess, Athena.* New York: Viking Press, 1972; New York: Penguin Books, 1982. 121 p.

A book for children.

**245.** *A Gathering of Spirit: writing and art by North American Indian women*, edited by Beth Brant (Degonwadonti). 2nd expanded edition. Rockland, ME: Sinister Wisdom Books, 1984. 238 p.

Originally issued as a special issue of *Sinister Wisdom*, no. 22/23, 1983. The contributors include well-known poets Paula Gunn Allen, Wendy Rose, and Chrystos. A spiritual awareness of history and nature infuses the poetry, stories, and narratives in this collection.

**246.** Gauthier, Xavière. "Why witches," *Bread and Roses*, 2(3):35–37, Autumn, 1980.

**247.** Gawain, Shakti. *Creative visualization.* New York: Bantam Books, 1982. 127 p.

A very helpful manual of visualization skills. While not specifically a part of feminist spirituality, this book is used enthusiastically by many women in the movement.

**248.** Gearhart, Sally M. "Future visions, today's politics: feminist utopias in review," in *Women in Search of Utopia: mavericks and mythmakers*, ed. Ruby Rohrlich and Elaine Hoffman Baruch. New York: Schocken Books, 1984, p. 296–309.

A critical review of feminist utopian fiction by Marion Zimmer Bradley, Dorothy Bryant, Suzy McKee Charnas, Charlotte Perkins Gilman, Marge Piercy, Joanna Russ, Rochelle Singer, Monique Wittig, and Donna Young. Gearhart examines these visionary societies with regard to collectivism vs. individualism, lesbian separatism, the response to male violence, the relationship to nature and appropriate technology, and racism. She also discusses her own *Wanderground*.

**249.** ———. "The lesbian and God the Father," *Body Politic*, no. 16, p. 12, November 1974.

**250.** ———. *The Wanderground: stories of the hill women.* Watertown, MA: Persephone Press, 1978; San Francisco: Allyson Press, 1984. 196 p.

A futuristic novel of a women's community in a California in which the men have taken over the cities and the women have retreated to the forests. Gearhart reshapes language to create a woman's world.

**251.** ———, and Susan Rennie. *A feminist Tarot.* 4th revised and expanded ed. Watertown, MA: Persephone Press, 1981 (first published 1977). 97 p.

An extremely useful handbook that re-interprets most of the cards from a radical feminist point of view. The Smith-Waite deck is used as illustration, with planetary and Kabbalistic associations given for each card, along with the feminist and traditional interpretations. Includes an introductory essay on how to do readings, and a bibliography.

**252.** Ghosh, Niranjan. *Concept and iconography of the goddess of abundance and fortune in three religions of India: a study on the basis of art and literature of Brahmanical, Buddhist, and Jain traditions.* Burdwan, India: University of Burdwan, 1979. 203 p.

**253.** Giles, Mary E., ed. *The feminist mystic, and other essays on women and spirituality.* New York: Crossroad, 1982. 159 p.

Seven essays from a primarily Catholic point of view. The title essay and Meinrad Craighead's "Immanent Mother" are the most relevant. Giles writes that a female mystic is by definition a feminist, in virtue of her seeking to transcend the roles and modes of thought of ordinary life.

**254.** Gilman, Charlotte Perkins. *Herland.* New York: Pantheon Books, 1979 (first published 1915). 147 p.

A utopian novel about three men—an intellectual, a romantic, and a macho type—who discover an all-woman society. Still a very enjoyable novel, *Herland* gives almost as much information about life in 1915 as it does about the ideal life under matriarchy.

**255.** ———. *His religion and hers: study of the faith of our fathers and the work of our mothers.* Westport, CT: Hyperion Press, 1976 (reprint of 1923). 300 p.

An early analysis of how male-dominated religion oppresses women.

**256.** Gimbutas, Marija. *The goddesses and gods of Old Europe, 6500 to 3500 BC.* Berkeley: University of California Press, 1982. 304 p. (Originally published as: *The gods and goddesses of Old Europe, 7000 to 3500 BC: myths, legends, and cult images,* Berkeley, 1974, but since only one of the chapters deals with male deities, with the new printing the title was changed to more accurately reflect the contents.)

An indispensable study of Paleolithic and Neolithic religion and culture in Eastern Europe. Gimbutas believes that in this area there was a matrifocal, reasonably high civilization, which she has termed Old Europe. This book is most valuable for the many illustrations of Goddess images and for the tracing of motifs from Paleolithic times to historical cultures of the Mediterranean.

**257.** Ginzburg, Carlo. *The night battles: witchcraft and agrarian cults in the sixteenth and seventeenth centuries.* Baltimore: The Johns Hopkins University Press, 1983; New York: Penguin Books, 1985. 209 p.

A translation of Ginzburg's *Benandanti,* first published in Italy in 1966, this fascinating work is based on his discovery of judicial records of inquisitors in the Friuli section of Italy, covering ca. 1580-1635. The *benandanti* (lit. "good walkers") were people who were in a sense "good witches" who went out at night to fight the spirits, or power, of the "bad witches" to ensure successful crops for the community. They were often accused of witchcraft, but they insisted that they were using magic only to fight the "bad witches," which so confused the inquisitors that almost all cases were dismissed. Ginzburg believes that the *benandanti* may have been a survival of (or devolution to) agrarian shamanism, thus supporting Murray's theory of pagan witchcraft, since they reportedly went into trances, healed, and found lost objects—all common shamanic activities. There are similar traditions of "good witches" fighting the "bad" ones all over Central and Eastern Europe, as well as in Asia.

**258.** Gioseffi, Daniela. *Earth dancing, Mother Nature's oldest rite.* Harrisburg, PA: Stackpole Books, 1980. 223 p.

Gioseffi reveals the secret that belly dancing was originally a Middle Eastern women's rite, celebrating the sacredness of sexuality and reproduction. The three main techniques of belly dancing imitate orgasm, birth, and letting the milk down from the breasts. Gioseffi traces the history of the dance from its matriarchal origins and connects it to New Age feminism. Includes instructions and many illustrations.

**259.** ———. "Lifting the veil of Isis," *Quest,* 3(2):70-76, Fall 1976.

An interview conducted by Esther Swartz.

**260.** ———. *The great American belly dance.* Garden City, NY: Doubleday, 1977. 182 p.

A humourous novel about a woman who discovers the Goddess through belly dancing.

**261.** Gipe, Karla C. *Daughter of the Lady Moon: a majickal Asian tale*; illustrated by Prairie Jackson. 1018 W. Pikes Peak Ave., Colorado Springs, CO: Moonwoman Enterprises, 1981. 20 p.

A Chinese tale of the Moon Goddess. Jackson has drawn many beautiful illustrations of the Goddess; her work has been printed throughout *WomanSpirit* magazine (see entry 722).

**262.** Glasgow, Joanne. "Revision of the sacred: reclaiming the world," *New Directions for Women*, v. 13, Nov.-Dec. 1984, p. 14.

**263.** Glass, Justine. *Witchcraft, the sixth sense, and us.* London: Spearman, 1965. 203 p.

An informative book on witchcraft, its pre-Christian heritage, and psychic skills.

**264.** Glendinning, Chellis. "The musical goddess," *Chrysalis* no. 2:11-17, 1977.

A startling and original look at the Goddess as manifest in Hollywood musicals (Carmen Miranda as Earth Mother).

**265.** Goblet d'Alviella, Eugene. *The mysteries of Eleusis: the secret rites and rituals of the classical Greek mystery tradition.* Wellingborough, Eng.: Aquarian Press, 1981. 128 p.

A translation from the Dutch.

**266.** "God created Woman in her own image," *Off Our Backs*, 1(21):1, May 6, 1971.

An editorial by the *OOB* Collective which introduces several articles on women and the Church, and women and witchcraft. Still a very clear argument against the sexist treatment of women by the Church hierarchy.

**267.** *Goddess Rising: a newsletter of womyns spirituality.* 4006 First Ave. NE, Seattle, 98105. Summer 1983-.

A quarterly newspaper oriented towards lesbian-feminist witchcraft.

**268.** *The Gods of Africa.* New York: Great Benin Books, 197-.

Issued by the Yoruba Temple, this work gives sketches of the goddesses and gods of West Africa, many of whom, like Yemaya the goddess of moon and sea, traveled to the New World with the slaves, becoming important figures in Black religions such as Umbanda in Brazil and Vodun in Haiti. This is one of the best descriptions of African deities from a Black perspective. The Yoruba Temple was an organization seeking to revive African religion among American Blacks in the seventies.

**269.** Goldenberg, Naomi. *The changing of the gods: feminism and the end of traditional religions.* Boston: Beacon Press, 1979. 152 p.

An excellent introduction for anyone who is not familiar with feminist spirituality, or does not realize its importance. Goldenberg writes of the challenge feminism represents to patriarchal religion and to father rule and of the new visions women are creating for themselves of God, Goddess, and spiritual practice. She sees feminist theology being utilized as a new kind of psychology based upon Jungian principles and on a respect for personal myth and symbol. Her book also examines the feminism of witchcraft, providing a succinct outline of Wiccan theology and its divergence from patriarchal religious tenets, in, for example, the lack of centralized religious authority, the concept of the union of body and spirit, and the sense of play within religious ritual.

270. Goodwater, Leanna. *Women in antiquity: an annotated biblio-graphy.* Metuchen, NJ: Scarecrow Press, 1975. 171 p.

Includes over 500 annotated entries, arranged by general works, Classical sources (female and male authors listed separately), and secondary sources. Covers women in Greece, Etruscan women, and women in Rome and the Empire. This is a useful source for articles on the existence of ancient matriarchies.

271. Göttner-Abendroth, Heide. *Die Göttin und ihr Heros: die matriarchalen Religionen in Mythos, Marchen und Dichtung [The Goddess and her hero: matriarchal religion in myth, fairy tales, and poetry].* Munich: Frauenoffensive, 1980. 252 p.

272. Graduate Theological Union, Library of the Office of Women's Affairs. *Papers, pamphlets, and books available at the Women's Resource Library, Women's Center.* Berkeley: The Center, 1973-74. 2 vols.

273. Grahn, Judy. *Another mother tongue: gay words, gay worlds.* Boston: Beacon Press, 1984. 324 p.

This book began as an investigation into the origins of modern gay culture—why is violet the color of homosexuality? why do lesbians wear pinky rings? what is the origin of the word "dyke"?—but it takes us into many other worlds, into the far past, and into the realm of pagans and shamans. Grahn found that in many cultures gay people have served as shamans, as it was believed that they could see into more than one reality, which indeed is the essence of shamanism. In our own culture lesbians and gay men still perform a shamanic role as they bridge the gulf between the sexes. Throughout the book Grahn weaves her own story as an emerging lesbian, living a life filled with pain, courage and pride. This is a most powerful and courageous book.

274. Graillot, Henri. *Le culte de Cybèle, mère des dieux, à Rome et dans l'Empire romain [The cult of Cybele, mother of the gods, in Rome and in the Roman Empire].* Paris: Fontemoing, 1912. 601 p.

A scholarly study of Cybele from her Cretan and Anatolian origins to her post-Christian survival.

275. Graves, Robert. *The White Goddess.* New York: Farrar, Strauss and Giroux, 1966 (first published 1947). 511 p.

In the wake of the horrors of World War II, Graves, already a highly respected poet and Classical scholar, sought to re-introduce the values of the Feminine into Western culture by revealing the contributions of the Goddess. The theme of this dense, difficult work is that "true poetry" in the Western tradition is ultimately dedicated to the Muse or Triple Goddess (Maiden, Mother and Crone) who with her son-consort was worshipped for thousands of years in Europe and the Near East. *The White Goddess* is an excursion as much into mediaeval Irish and Welsh poetry as into ancient myth, at times as hard to read as it is to describe. It requires a considerable amount of knowledge about Goddess-lore and/or the Celtic world (which Graves believed to have produced as a high a civilization as that of Greece or Rome), but it is well worth fighting your way through. For the beginner I would recommend first reading two or three books on Irish or Welsh literature and ten on the Goddess, or vice versa, and then have patience.

276. Gray, Elizabeth Dodson. *Green Paradise lost.* Wellesley, MA: Roundtable Press, 1981. 166 p. (First published in 1977 as: "Why the Green Nigger: remything Genesis.")

   A thoughtful, allusive book on the relationship between male domination of nature and sexism; human chauvinism; woman and nature as "The Other"; and how we can learn to be at one with the body, the earth, and each other.

277. *Green Egg.* St. Louis, MO: Council of Earth Religions, 1968-76.

   The most important Neo-Pagan periodical. In the seventies there was a long series of articles and letters on the concept of witchcraft as a primarily women's religion; a lot of traditional Neo-Pagans, male and female, found the idea very disturbing.

278. Greer, Mary K. *Tarot for your self: a workbook for personal transformation.* North Hollywood, CA: Newcastle Pub. Co., 1985. (Available from Box 7589, Van Nuys, CA 91409). 253 p.

   Greer uses Tarot as a psychological and mythic symbol system for personal insight and growth. Her illustrations are taken from many different decks, including Smith-Waite, Motherpeace, and Amazon.

279. Griffin, Susan. *Woman and nature: the roaring inside her.* New York: Harper and Row, 1978. 263 p.

   A visionary prose poem that celebrates and embraces woman's identification with nature and the earth, and at the same time is a ferocious indictment of male atrocities against women. A collective voice of women is woven throughout Griffin's litany of oppression, and in the end the feminine vision triumphs and reveals the spiritual power that resides within all women.

280. Grigson, Geoffrey. *The goddess of love: the birth, triumph, death and return of Aphrodite.* New York: Stein and Day, 1977. 256 p.

   A study of Aphrodite's origins, attributes, and persistence as male ideal.

281. Gross, Rita M., ed. *Beyond androcentrism: new essays on women and religion*. Missoula, MT: Scholars Press, 1977. 347 p.
Scholarly papers presented at a meeting of the Women and Religion Section of the American Academy of Religion.

282. Guadalupe. "Women's religion as revolution," *Sister,* 10(2):3, April 1979.

283. Hall, Nor. *The moon and the virgin: reflections on the archetypal feminine.* New York: Harper and Row, 1980. 284 p.
A poetic, healing book that looks at women's psychology via mythological figures. Hall, a Jungian therapist, uses psychoanalyst Toni Wolff's division of the feminine psyche into four quadrants: the Mother is opposed by the Hetaira or Companion to men; the Amazon or One-in-Herself is opposed by the Medial Woman who transmits wisdom (the Old Wise Woman). In Hall's interweaving of myth and psychology, Psyche is interpreted as a model for the woman who must learn to love; the maternal aspect is extended to cover all creativity.

284. Hallo, William, and J. J. A. van Dijk. *The exaltation of Inanna.* New Haven: Yale University Press, 1968. (Yale Near Eastern Researches, 3) 101 p.
The text of the first recorded poem in history, "Nin-me-šár-ra," a hymn to the Goddess Inanna by the priestess Enheduanna, transliterated from the Sumerian with an English translation and commentary.

285. Hansen, Harold A. *The witch's garden*; translated from the Danish by Muriel Crofts. Santa Cruz, CA: Unity Press, 1978. 178 p.
Hansen describes hallucinogenic plants used by witches such as mandrake, nightshade, and hemlock and explains the herbs used in the the witches' brew in *Macbeth.*

286. Harding, M. Esther. *Woman's mysteries, ancient and modern: a psychological interpretation of the feminine principle as portrayed in myth, story, and dreams.* New York: Harper and Row, 1976 (first published 1931). 256 p.
One of the most important and basic sources of woman-centered spirituality. Harding, a Jungian therapist, writes about the moon as mythic symbol and emblem of femininity and about Isis and Ishtar as Moon Goddesses and the Virgin as One-in-Herself. Her analysis of the psychology of women still has much to teach us.

287. Harner, Michael J. "The role of hallucinogenic plants in European witchcraft," in *Hallucinogens and shamanism*, ed. Michael Harner. New York: Oxford University Press, 1973, p. 125-50.

On the herbs such as henbane and atropine that witches used in making flying ointments. Harner is an anthropologist who is also an initiated shaman. In South America he worked among Indians who taught him the ritual use of a native hallucinogen.

**288.** Harrison, Jane Ellen. *Epilegomena to the study of Greek religion, and Themis: a study of the social origins of Greek religion.* New Hyde Park, NY: University Books, 1962. 600 p.

**289.** ———. *Prolegomena to the study of Greek religion.* London: Cambridge University Press, 1922; 3rd ed., New York: Meridian Books, 1955 (first published in 1903). 682 p.

Jane Ellen Harrison (1850-1928) was a Classicist who came to recognize that Greek and Roman religion exhibited many characteristics of "primitive" religions, such as totemism, king-sacrifice, and ancestor-worship. She also became aware that there is an undercurrent of goddess-worship throughout Classical mythology. She realized that a matrifocal period had preceded that of the Olympian gods, and that in the stories of the male gods the numerous assaults upon goddesses and nymphs were memories of the superimposition of god-worship over the original goddess-worship. Her work was not appreciated for many decades. These two books are long and require patience, for they are intended for the reader who has more than a nodding acquaintance with the classics. The *Prolegomena* was intended, in effect, to be read before one sets out to study Greek religion. Thus armed, the student would understand that the religion had not been always rational, intellectual, and male-oriented, but had gone through a period when it had more in common with African and Polynesian religion than Europeans might be willing to admit. *Epilegomena* (first published in 1921) is a short summary of Harrison's theories on Greek religion and its role in society; *Themis* (first published in 1912) continues her research into the formation of Greek religion, and treats such topics as Minoan religion and the pagan concept of the year; the original Olympic games, the Heraea, which were only for women; and the change of focus at Delphi from Gaea the earth goddess to Apollo the sun god.

**290.** Harrison, Michael. *The roots of witchcraft.* London: Muller, 1973; New York: Citadel, 1975. 278 p.

On witchcraft as the survival of prehistoric fertility magic. Harrison is greatly influenced by Murray's theories regarding the ritual sacrifice of the Divine King in England, Joan of Arc as witch, etc.

291. Hart, Vernette, and Lee Lanning. *Dreaming: an almanach of lesbian lore and vision,* v. 2. St. Paul: Word Weavers, 1983. 157 p.

292. ———. *Ripening: an almanach of lesbian lore and vision,* v. 1. St. Paul: Word Weavers, 1981. 158 p.

Collections of women's lore, statements of lesbian-feminist politics, drawings, chants, poetry, all seasonally arranged by the eight Wiccan holidays. *Dreaming* has contributions by many women. These are inspiring works of vision that are welcome contributions to the building of a lesbian sensibility.

293. Harvey, Steve. "Witch to go on trial," *Los Angeles Times,* pt. 2, p. 1, April 10, 1975.

A newspaper account of Z Budapest's prosecution for reading Tarot cards.

294. Haskins, James. *Witchcraft, mysticism and magic in the Black world.* Garden City, NY: Doubleday, 1974. 156 p.

This is an excellent source for the study of magic and paganism among Afro-Americans. The author traces the Black magical heritage to West Africa and describes the transformations African folk religion underwent under slavery in the U.S., Latin America, and the Caribbean. He includes material on Tituba, the slave woman who was accused of teaching witchcraft to the girls in Salem, Mass., and on the famous New Orleans high priestess of Vodun, Marie Laveau. The feminist spirituality movement is largely composed of white women; Haskins's book suggests that Black women already find a great deal of spiritual empowerment within their own traditions.

295. Hawkes, Jacquetta. *Dawn of the gods: Minoan and Mycenaean origins of Greece.* New York: Random House, 1968. 303 p.

A well-illustrated, well-argued study of woman-centered Crete and male-centered Mycenae by a British prehistorian. She makes a strong case for Crete's being matriarchal and has many unusual and thoughtful insights into Minoan and Mycenaean religion, particularly into ancient Greek patterns of culture.

296. Hawley, John S., and Donna Marie Wulff, eds. *The Divine Consort: Radha and the goddesses of India.* Berkeley: Berkeley Religious Studies Series, 1982. 414 p.

Papers presented at a conference at Harvard, June 1978, sponsored by the Harvard Center for the Study of World Religions. Radha is the consort of Krishna.

297. H. D. [Hilda Doolittle]. *Helen in Egypt.* New York: Grove Press, 1961. 315 p.

There was a Greek tradition that Helen of Troy was spirited away by the gods to Egypt, and that the Helen whom the Greeks saw on the Trojan ramparts was a mere illusion. This is a long poem, with prose interpolations, told mainly in Helen's voice. H. D. was devoted first to the Greek goddesses and gods, and later to those of Egypt. In her poetry she wrote frequently of magic and ritual and devotion to the Ancient Ones.

298. Heiler, Friedrich. *Die Frau in der Religionen der Menschheit [Women in the religions of mankind].* Berlin; New York: De Gruyter, 1977. 194 p.

On women as priests in ancient Western religion and in Hinduism, and the history of the idea of female Christian priests.

299. Heiligendorff, Wolfgang. *Der keltischen Matronenkultus und seine "Fortentwicklung" im deutschen Mythos [The Celtic cult of the Matronae and its continued development in German myth].* Leipzig: H. Eichblatt, 1934. (Form und Geist, Bd. 33). 100 p.

The Matronae were the Continental Celtic version of the Triple Goddess.

300. Heinsohn, Gunnar, and Otto Steiger. "The elimination of medieval birth control and the witch trials of modern times," *International Journal of Women's Studies,* 5(3):193-214, 1982.

The attack on women healers and the identification of their knowledge of birth control and abortion with witchcraft arose in response to the abrupt decrease in population that occurred in the fourteenth century due to warfare and the Black Death. More children were needed to further the economic and political expansion of Europe in the sixteenth and seventeenth centuries, so in their war against women's freedom the patriarchal secular powers enlisted the aid of the Church because of its longtime opposition to abortion and contraception.

301. Helck, Hans Wolfgang. *Betrachtungen zur Grossen Göttin und den ihr verbundenen Gottheiten [Reflections on the Great Goddess and her related deities].* Munich: Oldenbourg, 1971. 307 p.

On the Great Goddess in the Near East and Anatolia, from Neolithic times to the worship of Ishtar and Aphrodite. Traces the evolution of iconography.

302. Herberger, Charles. *The thread of Ariadne: the labyrinth of the calendar of Minos.* New York: Philosophical Library, 1972. 158 p.

On Minoan religion, especially its seasonal and lunar aspects.

303. *Heresies: A feminist publication on art and politics*; no. 5: Great Goddess issue, Sept. 1978.; 2nd. revised edition, 1982. 136 p.

A fine collection of articles, art, and poetry on the emerging Goddess movement that is an excellent introduction to the subject. Among the many contributors are Merlin Stone, Carol Christ, Lucy Lippard, and Mary Beth Edelson. This issue was so popular that it had to be reprinted.

304. Heschel, Susannah, ed. *On being a Jewish feminist: a reader.* New York: Schocken Books, 1983. 288 p.

In three sections: "Old Myths and Images" (the Jewish Mother, Lilith, the Jewish family); "Forging New Identities" (being a Jewish lesbian, women rabbis, joining the minyan); and "Creating a Feminist Theology of Judaism," which includes "Steps toward a feminine imagery of deity" by Rita M. Gross, "Feminist Judaism: restoration of the Moon" by Arthur Waskow (one of the two entries by men), and "A Spring cleaning ritual on the Eve of Nisan" by Lynn Gottlieb. Most of the authors are scholars, writers, or rabbis.

305. Hesiod. *Theogony, Works and days*; translated and with an introduction by Dorothea Wender. Harmondsworth, Eng.: Penguin Books, 1973. 170 p.

Hesiod was a Greek poet of the eighth century B.C. His *Theogony,* which is the relevant work here, is a long poem on the genealogy of the Greek gods that is considered one of the most basic and important sources for the Olympic myths. It clearly illustrates the transferral of cosmic authority from goddesses to gods, beginning with Gaea the primordial Earth Goddess and ending with Zeus.

306. Heyob, Sharon Kelly. *The cult of Isis among women in the Graeco-Roman world.* Leiden: Brill, 1975. 140 p.

Using Roman texts and inscriptions, Heyob describes the cult of Isis as it was practiced by women of all stations in life.

307. Hillman, James, ed. *Facing the gods.* Irving, TX: Spring Publications, 1980. 172 p.

Despite the male-oriented title, most of the articles in this collection are on the goddesses—Athena, Artemis, the Amazons, Hestia, Ariadne, "Red Riding Hood and Grand Mother Rhea." The articles look at the goddesses from a Jungian perspective; the authors include Christine Downing and Karl Kerenyi.

308. Hirvonen, Kaarle. *Matriarchal survivals and certain trends in Homer's female characters.* Helsinki, 1968. (Annales Academiae Scientarum Fennicae, series B, v. 152) 223 p.

**309.** Holderman, Elisabeth Sinclair. *A study of the Greek priestess.*
Chicago: University of Chicago Press, 1913. 54 p.
Originally written as the author's PhD thesis, at the
University of Michigan. She discovered that, as one might
expect, goddesses tended to be served only by women, and
gods by men. She attributed this to the fact that in primitive
religion the ministrant often ritually takes on the personality
of the deity.

**310.** Holmes, Tiffany. *Woman's astrology: your astrological guide to
a future worth having.* New York: Dutton, 1977. 301 p.
Astrological profiles tend to describe women in terms of their
suitability as wives and lovers of men. Holmes also considers
traditional astrology to be sexist since it equates male (fire
and air) with the positive and female (earth and water) with
negative. She shows how to combine one's horoscope with
feminist ideals.

**311.** *Homebrew: A Journal of Women's Witchcraft.* Box 6, Berkeley,
CA 94704.
Quarterly.

**312.** *The Homeric hymns*; translation, introduction and notes by
Apostolos N. Athanassakis. Baltimore: The Johns Hopkins
University Press, 1976. 107 p.
A collection of ancient Greek hymns, primarily from around
the seventh century B.C., which were attributed to Homer in
Classical times. The most important is the *Hymn to Demeter*,
which gives one of the fullest accounts of the story of
Persephone and serves to explain the origin of the Eleusinian
Mysteries. There are also shorter hymns to Hera, Athena,
Aphrodite, and Artemis.

**313.** Hörig, Monika. *Dea Syria: Studien zur religiösen Tradition der
Fruchtbarkeitsgöttin in Vorderasien [Dea Syria: a study of
the religious tradition of the fertility goddess in the Near
East].* Kevelaer: Butzon und Bercker, 1979 (Alter Orient und
Altes Testament, v. 208). (Thesis, Munster, 1978) 334 p.
A well-documented, scholarly study of the Great Goddess in
her many forms in Syria. Extensive bibliography.

**314.** Hornilla, Txema. *La ginecocracia vasca: contribución a los
estudios sobre el eusko-matriarcado [Basque gynecocracy:
contribution to Basque matriarchal studies].* Bilbao: Geu
Argitaldaria, 1981. 222 p.
Students of Basque culture have long been aware that the
Basques once worshipped a Mother Goddess who survives in
some religious and social aspects of the culture. An article by
Roslyn M. Frank, "The Basque Goddess," appeared in *Lady-
Unique-Inclination-of-the-Night*, Cycle 4, Autumn 1979, p.
66-77.

315. Hungry Wolf, Beverly. *The ways of my grandmothers.* New York: Morrow, 1980. 256 p.

     Hungry Wolf is a Canadian Blackfoot who describes the social and ritual lives of her older female relatives, collectively known as her "grandmothers."

316. Hunt, Mary E. *Feminist liberation theology: the development of method in construction.* PhD thesis, Berkeley: Graduate Theological Union, 1980. 209 p.

     Feminist liberation theology presupposes the subordination of women and the interrelation of sexism, racism, and classism with oppresssive social and theological systems. Hunt compares feminist liberation theology with its Latin American political model, and notes that the concept of theological "Universals" must be challenged by the disenfranchised. She constructs a philosophical method which she applies to the issues of sexist language in religion and to capital punishment.

317. Hvidberg-Hansen, F. O. *La déesse TNT: une étude sur la religion canaanéo-punique [The goddess T-n-t: a study of Canaanite-Punic religion].* Copenhagen: GEC Gad's Forlag, 1979. 3 vols. in 2.

     On Tanit (Anat) and her sister Astarte.

318. Iglehart, Hallie. "The spirit matter," *Off Our Backs,* 7(7):11, Sept. 1977.

     An article in defense of women's spirituality written in response to Marcy Rein's criticism (see entry 553). Iglehart insists that women's spirituality is not just an escapist movement but in fact supports and promotes political change.

319. ———. "The unnatural divorce of spirituality and politics," *Quest,* 4(3):12–24, Summer 1978.

     Iglehart considers the criticism of women's spirituality to be the residue of a patriarchal, dualistic worldview. Patriarchal religion re-inforces oppression as well as creates it; therefore it is necessary for women to recreate religion. She advocates meditation and alternative healing as tools that empower women to challenge sexism.

320. ———. *Womanspirit: a guide to women's wisdom.* San Francisco: Harper and Row, 1983. 176 p.

     An accessible, helpful introduction to feminist spirituality, serving as a manual of practice. Iglehart gives practical advice, meditations, and exercises, and describes her own spiritual history.

321. ———. *Womanspirit meditations* [cassette]. Berkeley, CA: Women in Spiritual Education, 1984. 60 min.

63

Guided meditations adapted from *Womanspirit* by Iglehart
and Marcellina Martin, accompanied by harp music performed
by Georgia Kelly.

322. *Immaculate and powerful: the female in sacred image and social
reality.* Edited by Clarissa W. Atkinson, et al. Boston:
Beacon Press, 1985. (Harvard Women's Studies in Religion
Series, 1) 330 p.

A collection of essays on woman's role in sacrality from
Ancient Israel to Tibetan Buddhism, including figures such as
the Virgin Mary and St. Augustine's mother, St. Monica.

323. James, Edwin Oliver. *The cult of the Mother-Goddess: an
archaeological and documentary study.* New York: Praeger,
1959. 300 p.

An excellent, thorough treatment of the Goddess in the
ancient world. Describes the characteristics of fertility religion
in Indo-European civilization, with chapters on Paleolithic
figurines, the Goddess in Mesopotamia, Egypt, Palestine,
Anatolia, India, Crete, Greece, and Rome. Having established
the nature and forms of Goddess-worship in the ancient world,
James traces pre-Christian imagery and beliefs surviving in
the veneration of the Virgin Mary. There is also a chapter on
the relationship between the Mother Goddess and the Son-
Consort. This book is one of the best places to start when
investigating ancient Goddess religion.

324. ———. *The tree of life: an archaeological study.* Leiden: Brill,
1966. (Studies in the history of religions; supplement to
*Numen,* 11). 293 p.

A study of this symbol in Near Eastern and Egyptian
religion. Chapter 6 focuses on the Goddess.

325. Jaynes, Julian. *The origins of consciousness in the breakdown
of the bicameral mind.* Boston: Houghton Mifflin, 1977.
495 p.

On the psychology of the right and left brains and non-
rational states, especially as they relate to religion and
mythology throughout history. Proponents of New Age
psychology, who include many people who honor the Goddess,
have sought to re-establish the importance of the relational
functions of the right side of the brain.

326. Jenness, Diamond. *The corn goddess and other tales from
Indian Canada.* 2nd ed. Ottawa: National Museum of Canada,
1975. (Bulletin no. 141; Anthropological Series no. 39) 111 p.

327. Jolly, Margaret. "Matriarchy: myth and history," *Refractory
Girl: A Women's Study Journal* (Chippendale, Australia), no.

11, p. 308, June 1976. (On microfilm as part of the Herstory Collection, published by the Women's History Research Center, Berkeley.)

**328.** Jones, Georgia. "God and Mother Nature," *Off Our Backs*, 1(21):5, May 6, 1971.

An early article on witchcraft as the first feminist movement and Joan of Arc as a feminist/Amazon model.

**329.** Jong, Erica. *Witches*; illustrated by Joseph A. Smith. New York: Abrams, 1981. 176 p.

A popular study of the history of witchcraft. The text supports the feminist view of witches as free women who were practitioners of traditional psychic skills, but readers may find Jong's treatment and especially the many illustrations of nude young women to be superficial and exploitative.

**330.** Jordan, Susan. "Witch, virgin, hag and crone," *New Women's Times*, Rochester, NY, 7(9):14-17, Oct. 1981.

Jordan looks at these aspects of woman and Goddess from the perspectives of etymology and European folklore, revealing sacred connections to the Goddess.

**331.** *Journal of Feminist Studies in Religion.* Decatur, GA: Scholars Press, Jan. 1986-.

A semi-annual journal, edited by Judith Plaskow and Elisabeth Schüssler Fiorenza. The first issue contains articles on the Cretan Goddess and the Goddess in Tibetan Buddhism; contributors include Naomi Goldenberg, Carol Christ, and lesbian Episcopal priest Carter Heyward.

**332.** *Journal of Women and Religion.* Berkeley, CA: Graduate Theological Union, 1981-.

Biennial publication. Formerly published as: Newsletter, Graduate Theological Union, Center for Women and Religion, 1974-81; published by the GTU Office of Women's Affairs, 1974-77.

**333.** Justin, Dena. "From Mother Goddess to dishwasher," *Natural History*, 82(2):40-45, Feb. 1973.

From the worship of the Mother Goddess as the Creator of all life to the negative images of wicked stepmother and evil witch, there has been a long tradition of the denigration of women through myths and folklore. Justin traces this cultural overthrow of the matriarchal image all the way back to the Paleolithic Era and detects it in the mythology of Greece (Gaea to Pandora), Europe (Venus of Willendorf to fairy-tale princess), and the Near East (Mother Goddess to Scheherazade).

**334.** Kakati, Banikanta. *The Mother Goddess Kamakhya: or, Studies in the fusion of Aryan and primitive beliefs of Assam.* Gauhati, India: Lawyer's Book Stall, 1948 (reprinted, 1967). 83 p.

Many scholars have considered the Dravidians, India's pre-Indo-European inhabitants (Tamils, Telegus, and other peoples), to have been more matrifocal and Goddess-oriented than present-day Hinduism would suggest.

335. Kalmar, Hermine. *Les dames d'une autre histoire [The ladies of another history]*. Saint-Raphael, France: Editions Les Bardes, 1976. (Les Cahiers d'archaeologie prehistorique globale, 1) 111 p.

On prehistoric women and images of the Mother Goddess.

336. Kalven, Janet, and Mary Buckley, eds. *Women's spirit bonding*. New York: Pilgrim Press, 1984. 389 p.

Based on the Women's Spirit Bonding Conference held at Grailville, Loveland, Ohio, July 1982. Grailville has been the site for many woman-centered spiritual gatherings, conferences, and retreats, with participants as varied as Rosemary Ruether and feminist witches.

337. Kanter, Emanuel. *The Amazons: a Marxian study*. Chicago: C. H. Kerr, 1926. 121 p.

The author regards Amazons as real, not mythical, women. He believes that women formed an all-woman state in response to the rise of patriarchy, whereas previously men and women had lived together in a pre-capitalist Golden Age of harmony.

338. Kapelrud, Arvid Schou. *The violent goddess: Anat in the Ras Shamra texts*. Oslo: Universitetsforlaget, 1969. 125 p.

339. Kapera, Constance. *The worship of Kali in Benares: an inquiry*. Delhi: Available from Motilal Banarsidass, 1966 (reprinted from *Amrita Bazar Patrika*, Nov. 3, 1961, p. 64–102).

340. Karageorghis, Vassos. *The Goddess with uplifted arms in Cyprus*. Lund: Liber Laromedel/Gleerup, 1977. 45 p.

341. Karim, W. J. "Malay midwives and witches," *Social Science and Medicine*, 18(2):159–66, 1984.

An intriguing article for cross-cultural comparison with the mediaeval European wise women and the suppression of midwifery during the witch-hunts. Psychic protection of the mother and child is one of the skills of the Malay midwife. As in many other cultures, including that of Europe, personal antagonisms can lead to charges of witchcraft. Animosity may arise due to professional rivalry either against another traditional midwife or against one of the new government-trained midwives who are taking clients away from the village practitioners. (In Europe it was the professional medical elite who denounced lay midwives.)

342. Karlsen, Carol F. *The Devil in the shape of a woman: the witch in seventeenth century New England*. PhD thesis, Yale University, 1980. 429 p.

Karlsen shows that Puritanism had contradictory ideas about women and agrees that there were social stresses underlying the witch-hunts, but concludes that these factors were more complex than is usually recognized, the accused being more than just scapegoats or social deviants. She describes contemporary ideas about witches and how these ideas were reflected in the accusations, and explains the socio-economic and religious factors most likely to result in someone being accused and prosecuted.

343. Kechter, Becky. "Riding the seesaw: feminism and spirituality," *Scribe* (Portland, OR), 4(2):21, March 29–April 4, 1975.

Kechter describes her desire to unite spiritual yearnings with feminism, which she feels is particularly important for women. She briefly examines the view of women in Hinduism and in the Judeo-Christian tradition.

344. Keeler, Clyde E. *Apples of immortality from the Cuna tree of life: the study of a most ancient ceremonial and a belief that survived 10,000 years.* New York: Exposition Press, 1961. 68 p.

Keeler was an anthropologist who worked among the Cuna Indians of Panama, who are known for the wonderful needlepoint *molas* made by women. In this work he compares the Tree of Life motif in the Cuna religion to that of Mediterranean Goddess religion. There are a number of surprising parallels. Keeler believes that the Tree of Life symbolizes the placenta and umbilical cord.

345. ———. *Secrets of the Cuna Earthmother: a comparative study of ancient religions.* New York: Exposition Press, 1960. 352 p.

Keeler believed that the Goddess of the Cuna was not merely similar to but was identical with the Great Goddess of the Near East—that is, that the Cuna literally worship a form of Isis—and that her worship was brought to the New World by ancient Mediterranean seafarers.

346. Keith, W. Holman. *Divinity as the eternal feminine.* New York: Pageant Press, 1960. 194 p.

Holman is a Neo-Pagan who seeks a revival of feminine values in society and philosophy.

347. Kelly. "The Goddess is fat," in *Shadow on a Tightrope: writings by women on fat oppression,* ed. Lisa Schoenfielder and Barb Wieser. Iowa City: Aunt Lute Book Co., 1983, p. 15-21.

One of a collection of essays by fat women. Kelly points out that the first images of women—the Paleolithic feminine figurines usually called fertility goddesses—were of fat women, and states that fatness, far from being "unfeminine," is in fact an integral part of femaleness.

348. Kelly, Janis. "...And another part: power," *Off Our Backs*, 6(9):2, 24; Dec. 1976.

A report on Barbara Starrett's "I Dream in Female" lecture given at the New York Spirituality Conference held Halloween weekend 1976 at Richmond College, Staten Island, N.Y.; she also reports on workshops on menopause, healing, and matriarchy.

349. ———. "Interview: Ruth and Jean Mountaingrove," *Off Our Backs*, 6(5):15, July–Aug. 1976.

Ruth and Jean talk about their backgrounds and the origin of *WomanSpirit* magazine (see entry 722). Jean defends their work against charges of escapism.

350. ———, and Fran Moira. "New York Spirituality Conference," *Off Our Backs*, 6(9):2, Dec. 1976.

An introduction to several reports on the conference "A Celebration of the Beguines" held at Richmond College in 1976. The authors were impressed by the feelings of identity and strength women's spirituality can give women, but were critical of the Goddess-worship aspect and the over-emphasis on one's reproductive capacity.

351. Kelly, Mary B. "Goddess embroideries of Russia and the Ukraine," *Woman's Art Journal*, 4(2):10-13, 1984.

In her study of women's embroidery in the Soviet Union, Kelly recognised Goddess motifs in the needlework: what looks at first like rick-rack, on closer inspection turns out to be images of the Goddess with uplifted arms who first appears in Paleolithic sculpture. When Kelly mentioned this to a Soviet museum curator she was working with, he beamed and said, "For thirty years I thought I was the only one who knew that!"

352. Kerényi, Karl [Karoly]. *Athene, Virgin and Mother: a study of Pallas Athene.* Irving, TX: Spring Publications, 1978. 106 p.

The motherless daughter of Zeus is often a difficult goddess for feminists to accept. Kerényi points out that Athena is a very complex figure who, among other aspects, exemplifies a form of the Masculine within the feminine psyche. Despite her seemingly cold and unwomanly persona, the ancients often felt close to Athena and habitually called upon her for aid as they had called upon many a Mother Goddess.

353. ———. *Eleusis: archetypal image of mother and daughter.* New York: Pantheon Books, 1967 (Bollingen Series, 65; Archetypal Images in Greek Religion, 4) 257 p.

The Mother-Daughter mysteries were celebrated at Eleusis, near Athens, for over 2000 years, yet the inner secrets of the religious rites have never been fully revealed. Kerenyi attempts to unravel the mystery of the Mysteries as much as possible, given the fragmentary textual and archaeological evidence, through analysis of portrayals of the rites on vases and pediments, the surviving myths of Demeter and Kore/Persephone pertinent to the Mysteries, and contemporary accounts of the rituals by Plutarch and others. He also tries to decipher what were the articles carried in the sacred baskets. There are many photographs of the remains of the sanctuaries and temples, and reconstructed plans of the buildings.

354. ———. *Goddesses of Sun and Moon: Circe, Aphrodite, Medea, Niobe.* Irving, TX: Spring Publications, 1979. 84 p.

In Greek religion there are many lunar goddesses, but few feminine deities have a solar aspect. Circe and Medea were daughter and granddaughter of Helios the Sun; Aphrodite is associated with gold and brilliance; while Niobe, whose many children were killed by Artemis and Apollo, may represent the Waning Moon.

355. ———. "Kore," in *Essays on a science of mythology: the myth of the divine child and the mysteries of Eleusis,* by C. G. Jung and K. Kerenyi, Princeton: Princeton University Press, 1969, p. 101-55. (Bollingen Series, 22).

356. ———. *Zeus and Hera: archetypal image of father, husband and wife.* Princeton: Princeton University Press, 1975. (Bollingen Series, 65; Archetypal Images in Greek Religion, 5) 211 p.

Describes the origins of Zeus and his cult and the formation of the myths that make a "family" out of the god and and his many goddess-conquests and offspring. In the development of Greek myth Olympus becomes a heavenly state ruled by the father. Of most relevance to the study of the Goddess are the final two chapters, which deal with the history of devotion to Hera, who was worshipped at Olympia and elsewhere long before Zeus. Kerenyi interprets Zeus as originally having been the young brother-consort of the Great Goddess, like so many Mediteranean gods before him.

357. Keshavadas, Swami. *Cosmic Shakti Kundalini (the universal mother): a devotional approach.* Washington: Temple of Cosmic Religion, 1976. 112 p.

In Hinduism the creative force of the universe is sometimes imaged as the Kundalini, a coiling serpent. The life force or Shakti is also depicted as the Divine Mother. Kundalini Yoga is a method to release the creative divine energy that lies hidden within the psychic and physical self.

358. Kieckhefer, Richard. *European witch trials: their foundations in popular and learned culture, 1300-1500.* Berkeley: University of California Press, 1976. 181 p.

Examines the evolution of the witch-hunts, the kinds of charges directed at suspected witches, and patterns of prosecutions and convictions. In addition to chapters on folk magic, contemporary opinions on witchcraft, and the socio-economic contexts of the trials and accusations, there is a calendar of witch trials for the 14th and 15th centuries.

359. Kimball, Gayle, ed. *Women's culture: the women's renaissance of the seventies*. Metuchen, NJ: Scarecrow Press, 1980. 296 p.

Separate chapters on music, visual arts, literature, religion, and fashion. Interviews with Mary Beth Edelson, Kay Gardner, Z Budapest.

360. Knight, Gareth. *The rose cross and the Goddess: the quest for the eternal feminine principle*. New York: Destiny Books, 1985. 192 p.

Knight has written extensively on the occult, in particular on the Kabbalah. Here he writes of the feminine principle in Classical religion, Rosicrucianism, and Tibetan Buddhism, and gives advice on how men may discover the Feminine within themselves.

361. Koch-Sheras, Phyllis, Ann Hollier, and Brooke Jones. *Dream on: a dream interpretation guide for women*. Englewood Cliffs: Prentice-Hall, 1983. 240 p.

The dreams described are from many women and deal primarily with feminine issues and experiences: menopause, relationships, pregnancy. The authors use feminist interpretations and employ a process of working through a problem via dreamwork.

362. Koerber, Hans Nordewin von. *Kuan Yin, the Buddhist Madonna*. Point Loma, CA: Theosophical University Press, 1941 (reprinted from *Theosophical Forum*, July 1941). 10 p.

Describes Kuan Yin's character and traces her origins, in part, to the Greek influence on India during the time of Alexander the Great.

363. Kolisko, Lilly Moha. *The moon and the growth of plants*. Bray-on-Thames: Anthroposophical Agricultural Foundation, 1936; new edition: Bournemouth: Kolisko Archive Publications, 1978. 85 p.

A scientific study that supports many of the "old wives' tales."

364. Koltuv, Barbara Black. "Hestia/Vesta," *Quadrant* (New York: C. G. Jung Foundation), 10(2):57-65, Winter 1977.

365. Kooij, K. R. van. *Worship of the Goddess according to the Kālikāpurāna*. Leiden: Brill, 1972. Vol. 1. 196 p.

A translation, with an introduction and notes, of chapters 54-69 of the *Kalikapurana*: a text of Hindu rituals relating to the worship of the Goddess as Mahamaya, Durga, and as the fivefold goddess Kamakhya.

**366.** Kraemer, Ross S. *Ecstatics and ascetics: studies in the functions of religious activities for women in the Greco-Roman world.* PhD thesis, Princeton University, 1976. 239 p.

Kraemer compares the participation of women in Dionysian cult with women's conversion to early Christianity. In patriarchal society the only woman of worth was the wife and mother of sons. Those women on the margins of patriarchal society—childless, single, widowed, or the women who in other ages would be lesbians or witches—were particularly drawn to religions that gave them a sense of self-worth. The Dionyisan cult appealed to women because of its celebration of fertility and sexuality, while early Christianity, through its ascetic values, gave strength and dignity to those women whose lives were by necessity already chaste.

**367.** ———. "Ecstacy and possession: the attraction of women to the cult of Dionysius," *Harvard Theological Review*, 72(1-2): 55-80, Jan.-Apr. 1979.

**368.** Krämer, Heinrich [Latin name: Henricius Institoris], and Jakob Sprenger. *Malleus maleficarum [The hammer of witches].* Translated by Montague Summers. Suffolk, Eng.: J. Rodker, 1928; New York: B. Blom, 1970. (First published in 1487.) 277 p.

This was an important handbook for witch-hunters, written at the beginning of the Burning Times by two Dominicans. Advice is given on how to recognize a witch and how judicial proceedings should take place. The authors state that women are peculiarly disposed to seduction by the Devil because of our supposedly naturally sinful and lustful nature. They also declare that disbelief in witches is itself a heresy. Among the specific charges they level at witches were that witches knew about contraception and abortion and had the power to render men impotent. A most important book for anyone studying the great witch-hunts.

**369.** Kramer, Samuel N. *The sacred marriage rite: aspects of faith, myth, and ritual in Ancient Sumer.* Bloomington: Indiana University Press, 1969. 170 p.

The act of marriage between the king and the High Priestess as incarnation of the Goddess was one of the most sacred and widespread ritual functions of women in Goddess religion. In some areas of the Near East every woman was expected to lose her virginity by offering herself as a priestess to the Goddess of fertility and sexuality. In Hebrew the priestess who performed sexual rites was called a *qedesh,* which is usually mistranslated in the Bible as "harlot." Thus Jeremiah's mother and Jezebel were priestesses of this type. Sexuality celebrated as part of religious ritual is what is probably meant by the Biblical "abominations" of the Gentiles. In scholarly literature sexual priestesses are referred to as "hierodules," which is Greek for "sacred women," but is often mistranslated as "temple prostitutes," giving the impression of women hanging around outside the temple with a lot of make-up on.

370. ———. "The weeping goddess: Sumerian prototypes of the *Mater Dolorosa*," *The Biblical Archaeologist*, 46:69–80, Spring 1983.
Characterizes the Goddess who mourns the death of Dumuzi the dying shepherd, and who weeps for the destruction of Sumerian cities.

371. Kraus, Theodor. *Hekate: studien zu Wesen und Bilder der Göttin in Kleinasien und Griechland [Hecate: studies on the nature and conept of the Goddess in Asia Minor and Greece]*. Heidelberg: C. Winter, 1960. 192 p.

372. Kunik, Sylvia Hanna. *The discovery of ancient goddesses and feminine religious experience.* Senior thesis, Rutgers University, 1976. 143 p.

373. LaChapelle, Dolores. *Earth wisdom.* Los Angeles: Guild of Tutors Press, 1978; 2nd printing, with new introduction, 1984. 183 p.
The author espouses a religion based on reverence for the earth.

374. ———, and Janet Bourque. *Earth festivals: seasonal celebrations for everyone young and old.* Box 542, Silverton, CO 81433: Finn Hill Arts, 1976. 196 p.

375. Lack, Roslyn. *Women and Judaism: myth, history, and struggle.* Garden City, NY: Doubleday, 1980. 218 p.
Includes chapters on Eve, Lilith, the Semitic goddesses, and women in the Bible and the Talmud.

376. *Lady-Unique-Inclination-of-the Night.* New Brunswick, NJ, etc.; Cycles (i.e. vols.) 1–6, 1975–83. Annual.
A beautifully produced journal of women's spirituality (the title is one of the names of the Goddess in pre-Columbian Central America). Contains articles, poetry, and photography focusing on religion, women's history, and literature; contributors include Starhawk, Kay Gardner, Mary Beth Edelson, and Christine Downing. The final volume is devoted to women's altars. Back issues available from Kay Turner, Folklore Center, SSB 3.106, University of Texas, Austin TX 78712.

377. Lal, Shyam Kishore. *Female divinities in Hindu mythology and ritual.* Pune, India: University of Poona, 1980. (Publications

of the Centre of Advanced Study in Sanskrit, Class B, no. 7) 352 p.

378. Landrine, Hope, and Joan Regensburger. "Through the Looking Glass: a conference of myopics," *Off Our Backs*, 6(4): June 1976.

A report on "Through the Looking Glass: a gynergetic experience," a landmark conference on women's spirituality held in Boston, April 23-25, 1976. (For the proceedings, see the entire Summer 1976 issue of *WomanSpirit*.) The authors are extremely critical of the conference, which they considered pompous, didactic, and divisive. This article provoked many angry letters in the following issue of *OOB* ("Letters," *OOB* 6(5):32-33, July-Aug. 1976).

379. Langdon, Stephen H. *Tammuz and Ishtar: a monograph upon Babylonian religion and theology.* Oxford: Clarendon Press, 1914. 196 p.

On Ishtar and the other Babylonian and Sumerian manifestations of the Great Goddess. The author is very hostile to the concept of the hierodule, i.e. the sacred prostitute (see entry 369). Many women have discerned a connection between the suppression of sacred prostitution and the rise of male control over female sexuality.

380. Lantero, Erminie Huntress. *Feminine aspects of divinity.* Wallingford, PA: Pendle Hill, 1973. 32 p.

381. Larner, Christine. *Enemies of God: the witch-hunt in Scotland.* Baltimore: The Johns Hopkins University Press, 1981. 244 p.

A thoroughly researched sociological study of Scotland's experience with witchcraft, this book gives an analysis of the social and political factors involved and describes the types of women likely to be accused. Larner shows that the witch-hunts were a tool of a new ideology consolidating its power.

382. Larson, Gerald J., Pratapaditya Pal, and Rebecca J. Gowen. *In Her image: the Great Goddess in Indian Asia and the Madonna in Christian culture.* Santa Barbara, CA: UCSB Art Museum, University of California at Santa Barbara, 1980. 127 p.

A catalog of an exhibit held Apr. 1980-Jan. 1981.

383. Lauter, Estella. *Women as mythmakers: poetry and visual art by twentieth century women.* Bloomington: Indiana University Press, 1984. 288 p.

The author, a professor of mythology and women's studies, examines the modern mythology created by women writers and artists (e.g. Atwood, Kollwitz, Sexton), showing how new myths arise in response to social and cultural change. In contrast to Jung, she believes that archetypes are not universal, but are rather created and recreated over time as cultural perspectives are transformed. A well-researched, thoughtful work.

384. ———, and Carol Schreier Rupprecht, eds. *Feminist archetypal theory: interdisciplinary re-visions of Jungian thought.* Knoxville: University of Tennessee Press, 1985. 296 p.

Essays supporting the need for Jungian psychology to be cleansed of stereotypes and sexism. Jungian analysis is the school of psychology that has been most useful and supportive in linking the psychology of women with feminist spirituality; many of the most influential works on women and spirituality have been written by Jungian therapists. This collection includes a chapter by Sylvia Brinton Perera on Inanna's descent into the Underworld as a model for feminist therapy. Other essays look at dreams, visual images of women, and the religious dimension of archetypes.

385. Le Bonniec, Henri. *Le culte de Cérès à Rome, des origines à la fin de la République [The cult of Ceres in Rome, from its origins to the end of the Republic].* Paris: Klincksieck, 1958. 507 p.

A scholarly study of Ceres's origins as Italic earth goddess, her various festivals and rituals, and her eventual identification with Demeter.

386. Le Corsu, France. *Isis, mythe et mystères [Isis, myth and mysteries].* Paris: Les Belles Lettres, 1977. 318 p.

The history of her worship from Egyptian to Roman times, its spread to realms as far away as Britain, and her survival in European folktales.

387. Lederer, Wolfgang. *The fear of women.* New York: Harcourt, Brace, Jovanovich, 1968. 300 p.

A psychological study of the awe-turned-to-fear of women's power, beginning with the worship of the prehistoric Mother Goddess and covering such topics as menstrual taboos, woman as death and decay, the vagina dentata, witches, and the patriarchal revolt against the Feminine. Some of the author's attitudes toward women will now seem antediluvian, but his research brings to light many aspects of feminine sacrality.

388. Lee, Carol. "Matriarchal Study Group Papers," *Feminist Review* (London), 1979, no. 2, p. 74–81.

Excellent criticism of the standards of matriarchal scholarship.

389. Leek, Sybil. *The complete art of witchcraft.* New York: Thomas Crowell, 1971; New York: Signet, 1973. 205 p.

Although some Neo-Pagans have asserted that Dame Leek was not a hereditary witch, as she claimed, she did a great deal to publicize the Craft in the nineteen-sixties and seventies. This is an informative little book, not a manual but an exposition of Craft philosophy as Leek interpreted it, with interesting chapters on witchcraft and homosexuality, reincarnation, and living in harmony with nature.

390. Leemans, W. F. *Ishtar of Lagaba and her dress.* Leiden: Brill, 1952. (Studia ad tabulas cuneiformas collectas ab De Liagre Bohl pertinentia, 1, no. 1). 41 p.
    On her clothing and ornaments as they are described in Babylonian texts.

391. Leland, Charles G. *Aradia, gospel of the witches.* New York: Leo Louis Martello, 1971 (first published: London, 1899). 36 p.
    Supposedly an Italian witch's Book of Shadows or handbook. Highly influential in the witchcraft revival; perhaps the earliest source for the "Charge of the Goddess," which serves as the witches' creed. Leland (1824-1903) was a prolific author and bon vivant who became an expert on Gypsy lore. In this book he writes that he got his information on witchcraft from an Italian hereditary witch. He includes the legend of Aradia, daughter of Diana, who was sent to earth as a female avatar in order to teach magic to oppressed peasants.

392. Lerman, Rhoda. *Call me Ishtar.* New York: Holt, Rinehart, and Winston, 1977. 247 p.
    A humorous, rather raunchy novel of Ishtar come to life in modern America, inspired by the work of Lerman's friend Elizabeth Gould Davis.

393. ———. *The supremacy of women [cassette].* Ithaca, NY: Cornell University, 1974. 62 min.
    A lecture and reading from *Call Me Ishtar* given at Cornell in February 1974. Lerman discusses the Great Goddess in ancient civilizations, the female as the basic form in nature, and dealing with the men in one's life.

394. Lesh, Cheri. "Holydays of the Goddess," *Lesbian Tide*, 7(5):5, March 1978.

395. ———. "Moon Calendars," *Lesbian Tide*, 6(5):28, March 1977.

396. ———. "Profile: Live Oak Womon, practicing Pagan," *Lesbian Tide*, 7(3):10, Nov. 1977.
    Live Oak Womon is a Black lesbian witch from California who has contributed to Z Budapest's *Holy Book of Women's Mysteries.* She wishes to reclaim African matriarchal religion, and in the interview explains that feminist politics and spirituality are inextricably linked.

**397.** ———. "Wicca is rebellion, not mysticism," *Lesbian Tide*, 6(5):19, March 1977.

**398.** Le Sueur, Meridel. *Rites of ancient ripening.* Minneapolis: Vanilla Press, 1975. 57 p.

Poems, mostly told in the voices of Native American women mourning the loss of the land and in the voice of the Goddess as Earth.

**399.** Lethbridge, Thomas C. *Witches: investigating an ancient religion.* New York: Citadel, 1968. 162 p.

An interesting and witty book on the pagan origins of witchcraft, prehistoric religion, and the Mother Goddess in Great Britain.

**400.** Levy, Gertrude Rachel. *The gate of horn: a study of the religious conceptions of the Stone Age and their influence upon European thought.* Atlantic Heights, NJ: Humanities Press, 1968 (reprint of 1948). 349 p.

An excellent study of ancient religion from the Paleolithic Era to the Greek mystery religions; Levy has amassed a considerable amount of information on the Great Mother. Covers the eras of the cave-dwellers, the Neolithic, Megalithic, and Bronze Ages, Crete, and the Greek Mysteries. Many illustrations of sacred motifs.

**401.** "Lilith: the creation of the first woman," *Off Our Backs*, 2(6):14-15, Feb. 1972.

The text of the Lilith myth accompanied by a drawing.

**402.** Lindsay, Jack. *Helen of Troy: woman and goddess.* Totowa NJ: Rowman and Littlefield, 1974. 448 p.

On the character of Helen in Greek literature, her origins as earth-mother, and her connection to Kore.

**403.** Lindsey, Karen. "Feminist spirituality," *State and Mind*, 5(4):12-13, Nov.-Dec. 1976.

This article examines the conflict between feminist spirituality and feminist politics. Political activists criticize spiritual feminists for seemingly withdrawing from political consciousnesss, for having an elitist, middle-class worldview, and for female chauvinism. These charges are answered by working-class feminist witches and women such as Marge Piercy and Lindsey herself, who have found the Tarot and *I Ching* to be useful tools. Lindsey presents an honest and balanced discussion of the spiritual/political controversy.

**404.** Lippard, Lucy R. *Overlay: contemporary art and the art of prehistory.* New York: Pantheon Books, 1983. 266 p.

The "overlay" of the title is the superimposition of human culture upon the earth's physical face, an activity which under patriarchy arises from disdain for the earth rather than reverence for her. Lippard's analysis is focused on the motifs of megalithic and matrifocal art and their re-emergence in modern art.

405. Litman, Jane. "Bima: is Judaism a matriarchal religion?", *Lilith,* no. 10, p. 32, Winter 1982–83.

The author has written many articles on feminist Judaism, sometimes under the name Jane Litwoman.

406. Llywelyn, Morgan. *The horse goddess: a novel.* Boston: Houghton Mifflin, 1982; New York: Pocket Books, 1983. 439 p.

The story of Epona, a Celtic woman of the first millenium B.C., whose exploits as a warrior and healer ultimately cause her to be deified in the myths of the bards (the historical Celts did worship a horse goddess named Epona). The cover of the paperback edition may turn off the feminist reader by its gushy historical-romance packaging (and endorsement by Janet Dailey); in fact this is well-researched historical fiction.

407. Lone Dog, Louise. *Strange journey: the vision life of a psychic Indian woman.* Healdsburg, CA: Naturegraph Publishers, 1964. 68 p.

408. Lucian [Lucianus Samosatensis]. *The Syrian Goddess [De Dea Syria];* translated and edited by H. A. Attridge and R. A. Oden. Missoula, MT: Scholars Press, 1976. 61 p.

Lucian, who may have been the model for the hero of Apuleius's *Golden Ass,* was a Greek writer of the second century B.C. In this work he describes the worship of the goddess Atargatis in the city of Hierapolis in Phoenicia. Atargatis was another form of the Canaanite goddess also known as Asherah, Astarte, and Anath. This is still a good source for research into the Goddess religion of the Biblical Gentiles.

409. Luke, Helen M. *Woman, earth and spirit: the feminine in symbol and myth.* New York: Crossroads, 1981. 102 p.

A gentle, thoughtful work on the feminine principle as spirit, as fire, and as motif in myth and fairy tale. The author calls for a re-valuation of the feminine values of relatedness and nurturance, cautioning that even among feminists these values are often denigrated, so that achievement in the external world is always deemed of greater worth that a contemplative, caring life at home. Much of Luke's analysis is drawn from Christian and Jungian philosophy, but she also writes of Demeter/Kore, Hestia, and the tale of Rumpelstiltskin; she has an unusual chapter on the feminine principle in relation to money.

**410.** MacCana, Proinsias. *Celtic mythology.* New York: Hamlyn, 1970; new revised edition: New York: P. Bedrick Books, 1985. 141 p.

An abundantly illustrated work that provides a considerable amount of information on Celtic goddesses.

**411.** McCrea, Margaret. "Women and spirituality," *Rain* (Portland, OR), 9(4):11–12, April–May 1983.

A survey of several seminal works in feminist spirituality: *The Changing of the Gods*, by Naomi Goldenberg, *Womanspirit Rising*, edited by Carol Christ and Judith Plaskow, Carol Christ's *Diving Deep and Surfacing*, and *Unspoken Worlds: Women's Religious Lives in Non-Western Cultures*, edited by Nancy Falk and Rita Gross (San Francisco: Harper and Row, 1980, 291 p.). McCrea makes her literary journey a very personal one.

**412.** McDonald, Sharon. "Z Budapest, witch in progress," *Lesbian Tide*, 9(5):6–7, March–April 1980.

Z describes her life from her girlhood during the Hungarian revolution to her coming out as a lesbian-feminist witch.

**413.** McDonough, Sheila. "Women and religion," *Atlantis* (Wolfville, Nova Scotia), 4(2):163–69, Spring 1979.

A critique of feminist theology, primarily that of post-Christian feminist theologians such as Rosemary Ruether, Mary Daly, and Sheila Collins. McDonough points out that in many ways the very concept of theology is ethnocentric and intolerant, since it assumes that philosophical questions posed from a Western, monotheistic perspective are universal in application.

**414.** McFarland, Morgan. "Witchcraft: the art of remembering," *Quest*, 1(4):41–48, Spring 1975.

This Dianic witch describes witchcraft as ancient women's religion.

**415.** Macha. "Female universe," *Goodbye to All That*, no. 30, p. 11, Spring 1972.

**416.** ———. "Female universe: male usurper," *Goodbye to All That*, no. 32, p. 3, Sept. 15, 1972.

**417.** McHargue, Georgess. *Meet the witches.* New York: Lippincott, 1984. 119 p.

An intelligent children's book on the history of witchcraft that describes the Craft's pagan and primitive origins and its past and present manifestations, without sensationalizing the subject.

**418.** MacKenzie, Nancy. *Palmistry for women.* New York, Warner, 1973. 171 p.

The author uses character traits revealed by the hand to give women advice about careers they might pursue.

419. Mackey, Mary. *The last warrior queen*. New York: Seaview, 1983. 240 p.

A novel about Inanna, a woman from a nomadic Mesopotamian tribe, who travels to a matriarchal pre-Sumerian city-state. Devoted to the Goddess, she becomes Queen, and must battle against the enemies of her religion and her nation.

420. MacLagan, Robert C. *Our ancestors: Scots, Picts, and Cymry and what their traditions tell us*. London: T. N. Foulic, 1913. 447 p.

The legacy of Celtic pre-Christian nature religion and Goddess worship in Great Britain.

421. MacNeill, Máire. *The festival of Lughnasa: a study of the survival of the Celtic festival of the beginning of harvest*. London: Oxford University Press, 1962. 697 p.

The definitive study of this Sabbat (Lammas, Aug. 1), as it was and is observed in Ireland, providing its mythic and folkloric background.

422. McNelly, Geraldine Day. "Women of the Celtic Tuath," in *Women in Search of Utopia: mavericks and mythmakers*, ed. Ruby Rohrlich and Elaine Hoffman Baruch. New York: Schocken Books, 1984, p. 21-29.

*Tuath* is the Old Irish word for people or tribe. McNelly gives us a visionary description of women in ancient Irish society and a selection from the Irish epic the *Táin Bó Cuailgne*: the argument between Medb, Queen of Connaught and her consort Ailill over which which partner has supremacy in marriage.

423. Madsen, Catherine. *The greengathering feast*. Box 591, E. Lansing, MI 48823: Tea Rose Press, 1981.

A songbook to accompany *The Patience of Love*, an album by Madsen and the Greater Lansing Spinsters Guild (Wormwood 001). This collection of pagan, woman-loving, nature-loving folk songs includes commentaries by the composers and performers.

424. Maity, Pradyot Kumar. *The goddess Bargabhima: a study*. Calcutta: Punthi Pustak; Indian Publications, 1971. 55 p.

Bargabhima is a Bengali folk goddess.

425. ———. *Historical studies in the cult of the Goddess Manasa: a socio-cultural study*. Calcutta, Punthi Pustak, 1966. (First written as a PhD thesis, School of African and Oriental Studies, University of London, 1964, with title: *The early history of the cult of the goddess Manasa*.) 377 p.

Manasa is a Bengali snake goddess of pre-Aryan—i.e., pre-patriarchal—origin.

426. Marconi, Momolina. "Melissa, dea cretese [Melissa, Cretan goddess]," *Athenaeum* (Pavia), new series, v. 18, 1940, p. 164-78.

The Goddess in bee form originated in Crete and can also be seen at Delphi and Ephesus.

427. Mariechild, Diane. *Crystal visions: nine meditations for personal & planetary peace; with drawings by Lynn E. Alden.* Trumansburg, NY: Crossing Press, 1985. 125 p.

Diane has been exploring the psychic realm within a feminist context for over a decade. Recently she has been studying with Dhyani Ywahoo, a Cherokee woman who is passing on the Native wisdom taught to her by older relatives. Some of the meditations were given to Diane by Dhyani, who has written the preface. Diane's message is that we cannot achieve international peace if we do not have peace within ourselves and with our family and friends. The language of the book is woman-centered, and several meditations contain images of the Compassionate Great Mother. Each meditation is followed by several blank pages intended for the reader's thoughts and observations.

428. ———. *Mother wit: a feminist guide to psychic development.* Trumansburg, NY: Crossing Press, 1981. 155 p.

An outstanding guide for women exploring their own spirituality. Contains many exercises for psychic work and guided meditations, with chapters on chakras, past lives, ritual, and psychic skills for children.

429. ———. *Womancraft.* Boston: Mariechild, 1976. 46 p.

The forerunner of *Mother Wit*; a collection of guided meditations.

430. Martello, Leo. *Witchcraft: the Old Religion.* Secaucus, NJ: University Books, 1974. 287 p.

An introduction to witchcraft as the survival of European paganism. Martello, a witch of the Sicilian tradition, has long supported the equality of the sexes within the Craft, and in the sixties and seventies was active in championing religious freedom for witches. In this work he bluntly condemns Christian prejudice against witchcraft, describes the workings of the Craft, the Goddess and God, and includes an interview with a Craft priestess and priest and a bibliographic essay on the literature of witchcraft and Neo-Paganism.

431. *The Matriarchist.* Box 247, Pratt Station, Brooklyn, NY 11205. Periodical devoted to matriarchal religion.

**432.** Matriarchy Study Group. *The Goddess Shrew.* London: the Group, 1977.

A special issue (April 1977) of the Group's publication *Shrew.*

**433.** ———. *Matriarchy newsletter.* c/o Sisterwrite Bookshop, 190 Upper St., London N1, U.K.

**434.** ———. *Menstrual taboos.* Flat 6, 15 Guilford St., London WC1: The Group, ca. 1977. 24 p.

The authors describe menstrual taboos found in traditional cultures as a form of misogyny. Originally, however, menstruation was regarded as a source of holiness and power for women. They trace the nearly universal observation of a periodic day of rest to women's retreats during menstruation.

**435.** ———. *Politics of matriarchy.* London: The Group, 1979? 59 p.

A fine collection of poetry, art, and articles on the Goddess and matriarchy. The authors discuss matriarchy as a political system in both its past and future forms, and issues of women and power. There are also articles on Eleusis, ancient Ireland, and the Maoris of New Zealand.

**436.** Mellaart, James. *Çatal Hüyük: a Neolithic town in Anatolia.* New York: McGraw Hill, 1967. 232 p.

This ten-thousand-year-old town is believed by many to be part of a verifiable matriarchy; matriarchy or no, Mellaart's work shows that urbanization did not inevitably mean the oppression of women. The archaeological evidence suggests that women had a high place in religion and culture: the special care given to the burial of women and children implies a matrilineal, matrilocal society in which women directed the religious rites. Every house had its shrine to the Goddess, who is recognizable as Mother Goddess and as Death Goddess in vulture form. The city's inhabitants were agrarian and apparently peaceful for many centuries, as long as the city stood. Researchers looking for a Goddess-centered matriarchy in the Near East usually start here.

**437.** Mellor, Ronald. *Thea Romae: the worship of the Goddess Roma in the Greek world.* Göttingen: Vandenhoeck and Ruprecht, 1975. 234 p.

Instituted by the Romans, the cult of Roma served as a bridge between the Hellenistic world and the Roman imperial cult. Once the imperial cult was established, the worship of Roma faded out of existence—almost. Like the adoration of the Virgin Mary, the Roma cult is an instance of patriarchal co-optation of the need to reverence the Feminine.

**438.** Melton, J. Gordon. *Magic, witchcraft, and paganism in America: a bibliography.* New York: Garland, 1982. 229 p.

An unannotated bibliography of some 1500 entries that covers all aspects of magic and paganism, feminist and non-feminist. The entries are divided into sections such as Witchcraft, Ritual Magic, Voodoo, etc., with a chapter on Feminist Wicca, p. 131-36, which concentrates exclusively on the feminist branch of traditional witchcraft. There are several sections on the traditions of people of color. Many of the items listed are pamphlets issued by various Neo-Pagan authors and organizations, and are kept at the author's Institute for the Study of American Religion, Box 1311, Evanston, IL 60201.

**439.** ———. "Witchcraft: an insider's view," *Christianity Today*, 27(16):22-25, Oct. 21, 1983.

A sympathetic article on modern Neo-Paganism. Melton is a Methodist minister who takes Neo-Paganism seriously as a religion in its own right. Rather than trying to stamp out witchcraft, he believes that Christians should only try to convert by setting a good example.

**440.** Merchant, Carolyn. *The death of nature: women, ecology and the scientific revolution.* San Francisco: Harper and Row, 1980. 348 p.

An insightful look at the concurrent rise of the philosophy of male domination over women and human control of nature in the sixteenth and seventeenth centuries. The scientific revolution fostered the image of nature as a machine with separate parts, rather than a living organism. Because women had long been identified with the natural world, women's freedom was considered to be synonymous with chaos, strict control over women's lives being thought vital for the preservation of society—a belief that is still very much alive today in anti-feminist circles. Merchant perceives the witch-hunts to be an expression of this deep-seated fear of women.

**441.** Merck, Mandy. "The city's achievements, the patriotic Amazonomachy and Ancient Athens," in *Tearing the veil: essays on femininity*, ed. Susan Lipschitz. Boston: Routledge and Kegan Paul, 1978, p. 95-115.

On the Amazon myths, the war against the Amazons as a symbol of Athenian patriotism and triumph of phallocentrism, and the relevance of Amazons to feminist thought.

**442.** Mestel, Sherry, ed. *Earth rites.* Vol. 1: *Herbal remedies*; vol. 2: *Rituals.* Brooklyn: Earth Rites Press, 1978-81.

Contributions by many women. The herbal remedies are arranged by physical complaint and include some magical recipes; the rituals are creative and are drawn from many traditions.

**443.** Michell, John F. *The Earth spirit: its ways, shrines, and mysteries.* New York: Crossroad, 1975. 96 p.

An essay on the history of the belief in the sacredness of the earth, usually identified with the feminine, introduces many pages of illustrations of sacred mounds, hills, caves, fairy paths, and grottoes in Celtic, Chinese, Native American, Mediterranean, and other realms.

**444.** Miller, David L. *The new polytheism: rebirth of the gods and goddesses.* New York: Harper and Row, 1974. 86 p.

A professor of religion influenced by Jung, Miller believes that polytheism is a healthier and more relevant theology for today. He calls for a revival of polytheism based on Greek models as a means to integrate the psyche's many facets and as an acknowledgement of a reality that is multi-layered.

**445.** Mimi. "Gynocide and theocracy," *Off Our Backs*, 5(4):12, April 1975.

**446.** Mimoso-Ruiz, Duarte. *Médée antique et moderne: aspects rituels et mythe [Medea, ancient and modern: ritual aspects and myth].* Paris: Edition Ophrys, 1982. 247 p.

On Medea as woman and goddess. The author analyzes her mythic adventures and points out that, like the Amazon, Medea is a model of the woman who will not be tamed by patriarchal marriage. Fascination with her image as woman in revolt has made her the subject of hundreds of plays, novels, films, and operas, which are listed in an appendix.

**447.** *The Moira handbook: a technique for breaking the time barrier.* Oxford, Eng.: The Madrians, Silver Chalice, n.d.

The Madrians are a modern Goddess-oriented group of women in England.

**448.** Mollenkott, Virginia Ramey. *The divine feminine: the Biblical imagery of God as female.* New York: Crossroad, 1983. 120 p.

This theologian writes that if the Good News of Christianity is to reach all people, then theological language must be used by which women as well as men can identify with God. Despite the lengthy tradition of the Biblical God as male, many feminine images of the Godhead can be found in both Testaments, such as Jesus comparing himself to a mother hen protecting her chickens, or to the woman who searches for a lost coin. There are also images of God as earth, wind, fire, and water; as a woman in labor; as mother animals; and as Lady Wisdom.

**449.** ———. "Biblical imagery of God as female," *RFD*, no. 35, p. 54, Summer 1983.

**450.** Monaghan, Patricia. *The book of goddesses and heroines.* New York: Dutton, 1981; published in Britain as *Women in myth and legend*, London: Junction Books, 1981. 318 p.

An excellent dictionary of goddesses and mythic female figures from all of the world's cultures. In the synopses of the Greek myths one clearly sees the pattern of male usurpation of female religion. Includes an extensive bibliography.

**451.** Monestier, Marianne. *Les sociétés secrètes feminines [Female secret societies].* Paris: Les Production de Paris, 1963. 265 p.

The secret society members discussed include druidesses and priestesses.

**452.** Monter, E. William. *The importance of witchcraft and the history of women [cassette].* Ithaca, NY: Cornell University, 1974. 60 min.

A tape of a lecture given on Halloween, 1974.

**453.** ———. *Witchcraft in France and Switzerland: the borderlands during the Reformation.* Ithaca, NY: Cornell University Press, 1976. 232 p.

On witchcraft in the Jura area, a region of many different cultures. The author observes that here witchcraft was treated much more leniently than in other areas of Europe: more people were acquitted, and the proportion of males accused was higher. However, those who were convicted tended to be the outcasts of society, especially if they were women.

**454.** Moon, Sheila. *Changing Woman and her sisters: feminine aspects of selves and deities.* San Francisco: Guild for Psychological Studies Publishing House, 1985. 232 p.

An examination of Native American myth and feminine psychology by a psychoanalyst who has written extensively on Navajo mythology; a fine addition to the growing literature of the psychology of women. Like Perera, Nor Hall, and Bolen, Dr. Moon uses mythology and goddess imagery with her women patients as a means of discovering the self and making it whole. Bolen and Hall have used Greek goddesses, and Perera the Sumerian Inanna; Moon utilizes the mythology of the Navajo and Pueblo (Anasazi) peoples, to whom she has been strongly attracted for many years. In her introduction she describes Navajo and Pueblo culture and society, the importance ascribed to the female, and the major goddesses and heroines, making comparisons to Western goddesses and mythic women. Each chapter gives a brief retelling of the native myths and stories of such figures as Changing Woman, Salt Woman, Spider Woman, and Snapping Vagina, followed by Moon's interpretations and the role played by these figures in comprehending the feminine Self.

**455.** *Moon Mirror.* The path. Box 1144, Aurora CO 80040: Cosmic Awareness Circles, 1984.

**456.** Morgan, Robin. *Going too far: the personal chronicle of a feminist.* New York: Random House, 1977. 334 p.

Of most interest is the chapter "Three Articles on WITCH: WITCH Hexes Wall Street; WITCH at the Counter-Inaugural; WITCH Hexes the Bridal Fair," p. 70–81. The articles, published between November 1968 and February 1969, describe the activities of the Women's International Terrorist Conspiracy from Hell, the earliest organization to unite feminism with witchcraft, albeit somewhat tongue-in-cheek. Also of interest is the chapter "Metaphysical Feminism," p. 290–310, in which Morgan admits that although she is an initiated Wiccan priestess she is also critical of what she sees as the lack of political acumen on the part of spiritual feminists.

**457.** ———. *Lady of the beasts: poems.* New York: Random House, 1976. 131 p.

Morgan celebrates the ancient and eternal power of woman as maiden, as wife, as Spider Woman, as witch.

**458.** Morgana. *The matriarchal art of belly dancing: a feminist perspective.* 207 Coastal Highway, St. Augustine FL 32084: Pagoda Publications, 1981.

Morgana is the founder of Pagoda, a women's spirituality center in Florida.

**459.** *Mother Church Bulletin.* Satellite Beach, FL, 1977–.

Quarterly publication of feminist religion.

**460.** *Mother-worship: theme and variations,* ed. James J. Preston. Chapel Hill: University of North Carolina Press, 1982. 360 p.

A collection of articles on the Mother Goddess in various guises: Guadelupe, the Black Virgin, St. Brigid, and mother-goddesses of India and Southeast Asia.

**461.** Motz, Lotte. "The winter goddess: Percht, Holda, and related figures," *Folklore: journal of the Folklore Society*, 95(2):151–66, 1984.

On the Germanic and Norse goddess who appears in Grimm's fairy tales as Mother Hulda. In mediaeval times food was offered to her during the Midwinter season, from the winter solstice to Shrove Tuesday. She is also the Lady of the Beasts, an old woman associated with the wild nighttime hunt, and guardian of nature, animals, initiation, and education.

**462.** Mountaingrove, Jean. "Love and a shoestring: hard work and miracles," *New Women's Times* 7(3):20–23, March 1981.

Jean writes about her life and work on *WomanSpirit* magazine. She explains the origins of the quarterly, its politics, and its collective mode of production; she writes movingly of her desire to make the magazine accessible to and reflective of all women.

463. Mukhopadhyay, Somnath. *Caṇḍī in art and iconography.* Delhi: Agam Kala Prakashan, 1984. (PhD thesis: University of Calcutta, 1981, with title: *Goddess Caṇḍī: a folk deity of Bengal*). 150 p.

Chandi ("the Fierce One") is an aspect of Kali who is widely revered in India.

464. Mulack, Christa. *Die Wieblichkeit Gottes: matriarchale Voraussetzungen des Gottesbildes [The femininity of God: matriarchal premises of the image of God].* Stuttgart: Kreuz, 1983. 367 p.

On the feminine principle in Kabbalistic mysticism, the polarity of masculine/feminine, matriarchal/patriarchal society, the Wisdom Goddess (Hokhma) in Jewish philosophy, and the relationship of Jesus to women. Highly informative for the feminist study of the Kabbalah.

465. Mullett, G. M. *Spider Woman stories: legends of the Hopi Indians.* Tucson: University of Arizona Press, 1979. 142 p.

Mrs. Mullett retells the Hopi creation myths and the adventures of the boy Tiyo and the Twin War Gods. Throughout the stories Spider Woman, the Hopi Creator-Earth Goddess, intervenes as the wise, all-powerful grandmother. The stories also show that, as in Crete and the Near East, the snake was important in Hopi religion.

466. Mullins, Joe. *The Goddess Pele.* Honolulu: Aloha Graphics and Sales, 1977. 35 p.

467. Münster, Maria. *Untersuchungen zur Göttin Isis: vom Alten Reich bis zum Ende des Neuen Reiches [Studies of the Goddess Isis: from the Old Kingdom to the end of the New Kingdom].* Berlin: Hessling, 1968. (Münchner ägyptologische Studien, v. 11) 239 p.

The role of Isis in Egyptian religion, her priestesses, and her relationship to other goddesses such as Nephthys, Nut, and Hathor.

468. Murray, Margaret. *The divine King of England: a study in anthropology.* London: Faber and Faber, 1954. 279 p.

Murray was a British Egyptologist who came to believe that the witchcraft of mediaeval and early modern Europe was nothing less that the survival of Europe's indigenous, pre-Christian nature religion. In this work she theorizes about the survival in England of the ritual execution of the Royal Victim or Dying God. She includes a chapter on "The Coven of

Thirteen," suggesting that important roles in English history have been played by groups of 13 coveners. Among putative witches she includes William II of England and Joan of Arc.

**469.** ———. "The female fertility figure," *Journal of the Royal Anthropological Institute of Great Britain and Ireland*, v. 64, 1934, p. 93–100, plates VIII-XI.

Murray divides the ancient figure of the divine feminine into three forms: the Mother Goddess, the "Ishtar type" (sexual model), and the "Personified Yoni," or Baubo/Sheela-na-gig image.

**470.** ———. *The god of the witches.* New York: Oxford University Press, 1952 (first published 1931). 212 p.

Although modern witches worship a Goddess as well as (or instead of) a Horned God, contemporary accounts from the time of the witch-hunts almost invariably mention only a male deity, called "the Devil" by the authorities of Church and State, and "the Black Man" by the accused witches. Murray was the first to point out the similarity between the horned, goat-footed folk deity and the Greek god Pan. Witches today define the Horned God as the lord of nature and animals who has been personified for thousands of years by shamans wearing antlered headressess. No extant physical description of the Judeo-Christian Satan predates the early Middle Ages, when Christianity was practiced side by side with native folk religion; therefore, it is reasoned, the Horned God is not the Biblical Devil but an entirely different and much older deity, the god of the old religion becoming the demon of the new. Judy Grahn (see entry 273) has speculated that the Black Man, who is described in contemporary testimony as the coven leader, was actually a woman dressed as a man.

**471.** ———. *The witch-cult in Western Europe.* Oxford: Clarendon Press, 1962 (first published 1921). 303 p.

In this groundbreaking study of European witchcraft, Murray emphasizes the documented persistence of paganism long into the Age of Faith. She gives a reconstruction of witchcraft rituals, initation rites, and coven structure and describes the pagan deities, the chief holy days or Sabbats, and the use of animal familiars. Murray's belief that mediaeval and early modern witchcraft was a survival of pre-Christian nature religion has been a controversial but highly influential idea in contemporary feminism. Her theory is so disturbing to conventional historians that they tend to dismiss it without bothering to offer opposing proof of their own. Nevertheless, her work has stimulated historians to examine the evidence surrounding witchcraft accusations in the light of folklore and anthropology and has forced scholars to consider the plausibility of the survival of paganism.

**472.** Mylonas, George E. *The "Hymn to Demeter" and her sanctuary at Eleusis.* St. Louis: Washington University, 1942. (Washington University. Literature and Language Series, no. 13) 99 p.

On the buildings and rituals of Eleusis as reconstructed from ancient texts.

**473.** Nadeau, Denise. "Lesbian spirituality," *Resources for Feminist Research/Documentation sur la recherche féministe,* Toronto, 12(1):37–39, March 1983.

A survey of the women's spirituality movement in the U.S. and Canada, its significance for lesbians, and lesbians' special spiritual values.

**474.** Nelson, Mary. "Why witches were women," in *Women: a feminist perspective,* ed. Jo Freeman. 2nd ed. Palo Alto CA: Mayfield Pub. Co., 1979, p. 451–68.

On the witch-hunts as a crusade for social control that began with the destruction of the pluralistic culture of the South of France and continued through the social unrest of the late Middle Ages and Reformation. Women were seen as dangerous and out of male control because they were limiting their fertility and entering the labor force in large numbers.

**475.** Neumann, Erich. *The Great Mother: an analysis of the archetype.* Princeton: Princeton University Press, 1963. 379 p., 189 p. of illustrations.

A classic work of Jungian scholarship, and a mine of information on the Great Mother as Goddess and as mythic figure. Neumann describes the feminine principle and its psychological and concrete symbology, the Goddess as Creator and as Terrible Mother, her relationship to the cosmos, to agriculture, animals, and fate. He interprets the Goddess-centered Mysteries as rituals of transformation and self-discovery.

**476.** *New Broom,* Dallas, TX, 1972–.

A periodical, now defunct, edited by Dianic witch Morgan McFarland.

**477.** Newall, Venetia, ed. *The Witch figure: folklore essays by a group of scholars in England honouring the 75th birthday of Katharine M. Briggs.* Boston: Routledge and Kegan Paul, 1973. 239 p.

Briggs is the leading authority on the folklore of fairies. The essays are on various topics of witchcraft and folklore in Western Europe, Japan, and the Third World. Among the more interesting entries are the editor's "The Jew as Witch Figure;"

"The Witch as Victim," by Geoffrey Parrinder; "Witchcraft at Some Prehistoric Sites," by L. V. Grinsell; and "The Divine Hag of the Pagan Celts," by Anne Ross.

478. Newton, Esther, and Paula Webster. "Matriarchy: as women see it," *Aphra: the feminist literary magazine*, 4(3):6–22, Summer 1973.

Two anthropologists examine the concept of matriarchy, starting with Engels and Bachofen but concentrating on feminist authors, particularly Beauvoir, Davis, Diner, Shulamith Firestone, Evelyn Reed, and three feminist anthropologists. They note that the anthropologists reject the historical existence of matriarchy and the non-anthropologists do not, but caution that feminist researchers must be willing to consider the ideas of women who work outside of academe and to confront their own chauvinism.

479. Nielsen, Ellen. *Kvinden i forhistorien: hvad myter og kultbilleder fortaeller [Women in prehistory: what myths and cult images tell us]*. Copenhagen: Hekla, 1981. 141 p.

480. Niethammer, Carolyn. *Daughters of the earth: the lives and legends of American Indian women*. New York: Macmillan, 1977. 281 p.

Niethammer looks at the ritual and secular lives of Native American women, arranging her material according to a woman's life cycle, beginning with childbirth and ending with old age and death. She also weaves legends and myths of Native American goddesses and heroines into the factual material. There are chapters on "Women of Power" and "Religion and Spirituality," and information on Native American lesbianism that is not found elsewhere.

481. Nilsson, Martin P. *The Minoan-Mycenaean religion and its survival in Greek religion*. New York: Biblo and Tannen, 1971 (reprint of 2nd edition, 1950; first published, 1927). 656 p.

A classic, comprehensive work that illustrates the Bronze Age civilizations of Minoan Crete and Mycenaean Greece. Apparently the Mycenaeans invaded or otherwise began to dominate Crete, which had been the higher civilization, sometime in the second millenium B.C. Cretan religion and civilization, which were Goddess-centered and possibly gynocentric, took on some features of the warlike, heroic Mycenaean culture, but Greek religion on the mainland remained strongly influenced by Cretan civilization. Nilsson discusses religious symbols common to both cultures such as the double axe, the horns of consecration, and the Tree of Life, as well as Minoan goddesses such as the Snake Goddess, the Lady of the Beasts, and the Mountain Mother. He shows that Minoan civilization did not die out with the fall of Crete to the Mycenaeans, but persisted within Crete and made many vital contributions to Classical Greek religion, including the goddesses Hera, Artemis, and Athena. The native Minoan culture and language survived in the eastern part of the island until ca. 500 B.C. Even today the Eastern Cretans have a noticeably different appearance from other Greeks.

482. Nivedita, Sister [Margaret E. Noble]. *Kali the Mother.* 2nd Indian edition. Mayavati, India: Advaita Ashrama, 1953. 104 p.

A devotional book by a disciple of Swami Vivekenanda.

483. Noble, Vicki. *Motherpeace: a way to the Goddess through myth, art, and Tarot.* San Francisco, Harper and Row, 1982. 276 p.

Noble and Karen Vogel designed a colorful new Tarot deck with a gentle, joyful character. Noble provides an explanation of women's spirituality and of the uses of the Tarot that is clear enough for the uninitiated to comprehend and appreciate. The designers' Minor Arcana suits depict people of four different ethnic groups, including African and Native American. Instead of King, Queen, Knight and Page they have Shaman, Priestess, Son and Daughter. In their Major Arcana cards, they have also made a conscious effort to include images of non-Western women. The cards themselves are round, to avoid the polarizing effect of interpreting the cards according to whether they are inverted or "normal."

484. Nolan, Susan. "Z and Helen sweep the nation," *Sister,* 6(6):4, Feb. 1976.

A report on the travels of Z Budapest and her co-covener Helen Hancken as they visited many women's communities and music festivals, lecturing on the Goddess and feminist witchcraft.

485. Nower, Joyce. "Mary Daly: toward a feminist philosophy," *The Longest Revolution,* 3(5):1, 10–11, June 1979.

An interview with Daly, who discusses her background and the philosophy she puts forth in *Gyn/Ecology*: the deception of women via language and myth, the atrocities enacted against women around the world (popularly sanitized as quaint "customs"), and the philosophical journey feminists must make. She also describes her concept of "Goddess."

486. Oakwoman, Amy. "Crafting a personal ritual," *Country Women,* no. 24, p. 24–26, April 1977.

The author describes the deep personal meaning witchcraft has for her as a feminist, and how she has utilized Craft techniques in her quest for self-awareness.

**487.** Ōbayashi, Taryōhen, Akiko Ono, et al. *Bokensei no nazo [The riddle of matriarchy].* Tokyo: Hyōronsha, 1975. 252 p.
On the history of women and the matriarchal period.

**489.** Obeyeskekere, Gananath. *The cult of the goddess Pattini.* Chicago: University of Chicago Press, 1984. 629 p.
Pattini is a goddess worshipped by Tamils, Buddhists, and Jains in Sri Lanka and South India. This is a detailed study of her worship, including many sacred texts. Most relevant is the second half of the book, which describes Pattini as Virgin, as Mater Dolorosa, and as wife of the Dying God.

**490.** Ochs, Carol. *Behind the sex of God: toward a new consciousness— transcending matriarchy and patriarchy.* Boston: Beacon Press, 1977. 177 p.
Examines the Eleusinian mysteries, some Judeo-Christian themes, and survivals of Goddess-religion evident in the devotion to Mary. Ochs seeks to transcend all dualistic thought regarding God, which extends even to the conflict between matriarchy and patriarchy.

**491.** ———. *Women and spirituality.* Boston: Rowman, 1983. 156 p.
How the events and character of women's lives can lead us to experience the Divine as manifest within us. Ochs uses motherhood as a model for numinous experience, with spirituality encountered in five stages: awakening, purgation, illumination, the dark night of the soul, and finally, union with the Divine. This experience has often been thought of as a journey; Ochs tells us to look at the present moment in our spiritual experiences rather than being goal-oriented.

**492.** Ochshorn, Judith. *The female experience and the nature of the divine.* Bloomington: Indiana University Press, 1981. 269 p.
This author looks at gender, sex roles, power, and participation in ritual, first from the Near Eastern polytheistic perspective and secondly from the Biblical, primarily Old Testament, point of view. She finds that although pre-Biblical polytheistic society was certainly patriarchal, gender as such was not a religious issue, since both men and women participated fully in ritual, as priests and as laity. However, with the Hebrew substitution of monotheism for polytheism the One God became imaged as male, which ultimately strengthened social patriarchy and excluded women from most ritual functions.

**493.** O'Connell, Margaret F. *The magic cauldron: witchcraft for good and evil.* New York: S. G. Phillips, 1975. 192 p.
A popular history of witchcraft and its social and political contexts, from ancient times to Salem. Gives spells, chants, and a guide to the Sabbats. O'Connell emphasizes the role of

women and the Moon Goddess, but also tends to take a negative view of witchcraft.

**494.** Oda, Mayumi. *Goddesses.* Berkeley: Lancaster-Miller Publications, 1981. 78 p.

A collection of powerful silk-screened images of the Goddess as an accessible and human figure. Oda's style is very Japanese but very contemporary; her Goddesses play the flute and ride bicycles.

**495.** *Of a Like Mind.* Box 6021, Madison, WI 53716. 1984-.

Quarterly newspaper with a goal of forming a network among spiritual women. Goddess- and Craft-oriented.

**496.** Okano, Haruko. *Die Stellung der Frau in Shintô: eine religionsphänomenologische und soziologische Untersuchung [The position of women in Shinto: a religious, phenomenological and sociological study].* Wiesbaden: Harrassowitz, 1976 (PhD thesis, Rheinischen Freidrich-Wilhelms Universität). 364 p.

An excellent source for the woman-centered study of Shinto. Ms. Okano first gives a detailed account of Shinto's origins as a gynocentric religion, the primacy of priestesses, and women's role in traditional and modern Shinto. She then describes the parts played by the Great Goddess, the Feminine Principle, priestesses, noblewomen, and empresses.

**497.** Okumuru, Yoshinobu. *Manshū nyannyan kō; Studies on Chinese goddesses of Manchuria.* Taipei: Chūgoku Minzoku Gakkai (Chinese Folklore Association), 1984. 2 v.

In Japanese. Reprint of 1940 edition, published in Shinkyō, Japan by Manshū Jijō Annaijo.

**498.** Olender, Marcel. "Aspects de Baubô: textes et contextes antiques," *Revue de l'Histoire des Religions*, 202(1):3-55, Jan.-Mar. 1985.

Baubo is the woman who, by unexpectedly revealing her genitals, finally made Demeter laugh and begin to re-awaken emotionally after the loss of Persephone. This article is a detailed study of the goddess of the (suppposedly) obscene and of the sacredness of female sexuality.

**499.** Olson, Carl, ed. *The Book of the Goddess, Past and Present: an introduction to Her religion.* New York: Crossroad, 1983. 261 p.

A collection of articles, mostly by women, on Goddess-worship in the Near East, Greece, Rome, India, China, Japan, Africa, and North America, from prehistoric times to the resurgence of feminist spirituality. Contributors include Rita M. Gross, Christine Downing, Judith Ochshorn, and Carol Christ.

**500.** Oriethyia. *Love song to the warriors.* E. Setauket, NY: Lenachild Press, 1980. 48 p.

Poetry that celebrates our Amazon and Goddess heritage.

**501.** *The Orphic hymns;* texts, translation and notes by Apostolos N. Athanassakis. Missoula, MT: Scholars Press, 1977. 146 p.

These are very old Greek hymns to the goddesses and gods, which have been attributed to the poet Orpheus.

**502.** Ortiz-Osés, Andres, and F. K. Mayr. *El inconsciente colectivo vasco: mitología cultural y arquetipos psicosociales [The Basque collective unconscious: cultural mythology and psychosocial archetypes].* San Sebastián, Spain: Ediciones Txertoas, 1982. 242 p.

The authors identify the unconscious with matriarchal religion and culture, and the conscious with patriarchy. The matriarchal element survives among the Basques, who are of pre-Indo-European origin, in their worldview and in their devotion to the Goddess in the form of the Virgin Mary.

**503.** ——. *El matriarcalismo vasco [Basque matriarchy].* Bilbao, Spain: Universidad de Deusto, 1980. 139 p.

On the matriarchal era in Spain.

**504.** Ortner, Sherry. "Is female to male as nature is to culture?" *Feminist Studies,* 1(2):5–32, Fall 1972. Also reprinted in *Woman, Culture and Society,* ed. Michelle Rosaldo and Louise Lamphere. Stanford, CA: Stanford University Press, 1974, p. 67–87.

A classic article which describes the patriarchal identification of women with nature, the primitive, and the untamed. Written as anthropology, this work became a cornerstone of feminist criticism of the patriarchal worldview, and ultimately of feminist spiritual philosophy.

**505.** Otto, Walter A. *Beiträge zur Hierodulie im Hellenistischen Ägypten [Contributions to the study of hierodules in Hellenistic Egypt].* Munich: Bayerische Akademie der Wissenschaften, 1949. (Its Abhandlungen, new series, no. 29). 74 p.

A scholarly study of the hierodule or "temple prostitute:" the priestess of the Great Goddess who gave spiritual knowledge to men through sexual union.

**506.** *The Owl.* Covenant of the Ancient Way, Box 161672, Sacramento, CA 95816.

Periodical of Neo-Paganism.

**507.** *Pagan-Occult-New Age Directory,* ed. Rhuddlwm Gawr. Athens, GA: Pagan Grove Press, 1980–.

Annual directory of Neo-Pagan and witchcraft organizations and circles.

**508.** *Pagan sexism?* N.p.: The Witching Well Education and Research Center, 1980. 6 p. (Held at the Institute for the Study of American Religion, Box 1311, Evanston IL 60201.)

**509.** Page, Eric. "Women's cults of antiquity: the veil rises," *New York Times*, April 30, 1985, pp. C1, C8.

A report on the excavation of sanctuaries in Southern Italy dedicated to Bona Dea, a goddess worshippped almost exclusively by women. Page interviewed several classicists, including Sarah Pomeroy.

**510.** Pagels, Elaine. *The Gnostic gospels.* New York: Random House, 1979. 214 p.

A very exciting book on the Nag Hammadi manuscripts, the first actual Gnostic texts to be discovered. Prior to their discovery some thirty years ago, researchers into Gnosticism had to rely on what anti-Gnostic Christian writers had to say about their beliefs and practices, so these texts are to Gnosticism what a genuine mediaeval Book of Shadows would be to modern witches. The texts are very revealing about the important role of the Feminine not only in Gnosticism but also in early orthodox Christianity.

**511.** *Parabola: myth and the quest for meaning.* Mt. Kisco, NY: Tamarack Press, 1976-.

This quarterly journal looks at the power and role of myth poetically, religiously, and psychologically. Readers will probably find any one of its issues interesting. Each issue is devoted to a particular topic (e.g. "Earth," "Sleep," "Dreams," "The Trickster") and includes texts of ancient and contemporary native myths. Of special interest are the Nov. 1978 issue (v. 3, no. 4) on "Androgyny," which contains articles on the Gnostic Gospels, astrology, and "The Older Woman as Androgyne" by anthropologist Barbara Myerhoff; and the issue devoted to "Woman," (v. 5, no. 4, Fall 1980), which has articles by P. L. Travers (author of the Mary Poppins books and a frequent contributor to *Parabola*), Helen M. Luke, Ursula LeGuin, Diane Wolkstein and S. N. Kramer, and Joseph Campbell, among others.

**512.** Passmore, Nancy. *The lunar calendar: dedicated to the Goddess in her many guises.* Boston: Luna Press, 1977-.

Like the great revolutions in France and Russia, the women's revolution has created its own calendar. The year is divided into the thirteen lunar months, based on the Celtic tree-alphabet described in Robert Graves's *The White Goddess*, and the days are arranged on the pages in spirals rather than straight lines. Each month is accompanied by an essay on the lore of the appropriate tree or shrub and an illustration of the appropriate Goddess. Passmore also instructs the reader in astrology and planting by the moon.

513. Patai, Raphael. *The Hebrew Goddess.* Philadelphia: Ktav, 1967; New York: Avon, 1978. 349 p.

An excellent work on the goddesses and divine female figures—Asherah, the Cherubim, Lilith, Hokhma (Wisdom), the Shekhinah—worshipped surreptitiously or openly by the supposedly monotheistic and patriarchal Hebrews. Patai also reveals the presence of the Goddess in the Old Testament. His work is a basic source for feminist research into Judaism.

514. Pearson, Karl. "Woman as Witch: evidences of Mother-Right in the customs of medieval witchcraft," in his *The chances of death, and other studies in evolution.* London; New York: E. Arnold, 1897, v. 2, p. 1-50.

On the origins of witchcraft as pre-patriarchal fertility cult. Also of interest are the subsequent chapters: "Ashepattle: or Hans Seeks His Luck," and "Kindred Group Marriage," for evidence of the survival of matriarchy and the Mother-Goddess, among other intriguing topics.

515. Pepper, Elizabeth, and John Wilcock, eds. *The witches' almanac.* New York: Grosset and Dunlap, 1971-80.

An annual astrological-lunar calendar, running from Aries to Pisces of each astrological year, accompanied by short articles on various aspects of witchcraft and the Mysteries.

516. Perera, Sylvia Brinton. *Descent to the Goddess: a way of initiation for women.* Toronto: Inner City Books, 1981. 111 p.

This Jungian analyst brilliantly and creatively uses the ancient story of the descent of Inanna to the underworld as a model for women's psychological descent into the depths in order to find strength and healing.

517. Perry, Deborah L. "Ceremonies celebrating life," *New Directions for Women* v. 13:12-13, Nov.-Dec. 1984.

518. Persson, Axel. *The religion of Greece in prehistoric times.* Berkeley: University of California Press, 1942. (Sather Classical Lectures, v. 17) 189 p.

An excellent introduction to Minoan Goddess religion. Persson seeks to show that there was a lively religious culture in the Eastern Mediterranean before the rise of Classical civilization. Many features of this religion were common to North Africa, Crete, Mesopotamia, and the Indus Valley. He describes Minoan and Mycenaean religion, with special attention paid to the illustration of religious rites on Cretan signet rings, the sacred vegetation cycle, and the theme of death and rebirth. He compares the Cretan goddess with her

Near Eastern counterparts, such as Ishtar, and examines the relationship between the Great Goddess and the Dying God; the Grecian debt to Crete in the veneration of Hera, Artemis, and Demeter; and offers a comparison to Norse Bronze Age religion. There are many excellent reproductions of Minoan signet rings, which have been a major source for our knowledge of the religion of Crete.

519. Pestalozza, Uberto. *L'éternel féminin dans la religion méditerranéenne [The eternal feminine in Mediterranean religion]*. Brussels: Latomus, 1965. (Collection Latomus, v. 79) 70 p.

On the *Potnia* or Lady, as the Goddess was often called, in Crete and Greece. Pestalozza points out that in the ancient world the common woman was able to identify with the Divine, who, like her, brought forth children and prepared food, and who was made visible in the cycles of the moon and the contours of the earth.

520. ———. "Selene e la mitologia lunare nel mondo religioso preellenico [Selene and lunar mythology in the prehellenic religious world]," *Acme: annali della Facoltà di Filosofia e Lettere dell'Università Statale di Milano*, 6(3):349-74, Sept.-Dec. 1953.

Although Greek texts referring to Selene describe her primarily as a moon goddess, there is evidence that in pre-Hellenic times she had a wider range of functions, being originally more akin to Gaea as primordial Earth Mother.

521. Petersen, E. "Die dreigestaltige Hekate [Triform Hecate]," *Archäologisch-epigraphische Mittheilungen aus Oesterreich*, vol. 4, 1880, pp.140-74; vol. 5, pp. 1-84 + plates.

Includes some interesting illustrations of statuary.

522. Philpot, Mrs. J. H. *The sacred tree: or, The tree in religion and myth*. New York: Macmillan, 1897. 179 p.

The Tree of Life or Moon Tree was an important symbol in Near Eastern Goddess religion and in much of pre-Christian Europe. Mrs. Philpot (her own name now lost to history) gathered together a considerable amount of information on such varied topics as the Dying God, tree-worship in Western Europe, and tree-spirits (usually female); she adds two chapters on European customs surrounding May Day and Christmas/Winter Solstice.

523. Picard, Charles. *Les religions préhelleniques (Crète et Mycènes) [Prehellenic religions (Crete and Mycenaea)]*. Paris: Presses Universitaires de France, 1948 (Mana: introduction à l'histoire des religions, v. 2, pt. 1: Les religions de l'Europe ancienne); reprinted, Paris: Cisalpino Goliardica, 1972. 332 p.

On the Mother Goddess and the son-consort in the Neolithic era and Bronze Age, and the Minoan-Mycenaean origin of classical Greek religion. Each chapter has its own extensive bibliographic essay, providing many additional sources for the further investigation of Greek myth and religion.

**524.** Piccaluga, Giulia. "Bona Dea: due contributi all'interpretazione del suo culto" [Bona Dea: two contributions to the interpretation of her cult], *Studi e Materiali di Stori delle Religione*, v. 35, 1964, p. 195–237.

Description of the all-women rites to Bona Dea, characterized by much wine-drinking and merrymaking, according to male Roman writers who also accused the women of sexual promiscuity with one another within the rituals. Bona Dea was known to the Greeks and Romans as "the Goddess of Women"; her Roman cult was borrowed from Greeks who colonized Southern Italy and Sicily.

**525.** Pierce, Tamora. *Alanna: the first adventure.* New York: Atheneum, 1983. (Song of the Lioness, book 1) 241 p.

This novel and its sequel (see next entry) are Goddess-oriented sword-and-sorcery stories for young people. In the first installment, eleven-year-old Alanna disguises herself as a boy in order to become a page and eventually a squire.

**526.** ———. In the hands of the Goddess. New York: Atheneum, 1984. (Song of the Lioness, book 2) 232 p.

**527.** Piercy, Marge. *The moon is always female.* New York: Knopf, 1981. 133 p.

Poems shaped by feminist politics. Includes "The Lunar Cycle," a group of poems based on the Celtic tree-alphabet calendar.

**528.** Pinkham, Mildreth Worth. *Woman in the sacred scriptures of Hinduism.* New York: AMS Press, 1967 (reprint of 1941 edition). 239 p.

Mrs. Pinkham was interested in the effect scriptural attitudes have had on the social, legal, and economic position of Indian women. Under consideration are texts from the earliest indigenous religion, before the first millennium B.C., to the period of the *Ramayana* (250 A.D.), including the Vedas, the Upanishads, the Puranas, and the Bhagavad Gita.

**529.** Plaskow, Judith [Judith Plaskow Goldenberg]. "Epilogue: the coming of Lilith," in *Religion and sexism: images of woman in the Jewish and Christian traditions*, ed. Rosemary Radford Ruether. New York: Simon and Schuster, 1974, p. 341–43.

A retelling of the story of the Garden of Eden which ends with solidarity between Eve and Lilith.

**530.** ———, and Joan Arnold Romero, comps. *Women and religion: papers of the Working Group on Women and Religion, 1972-73.* Revised edition. Chambersburg, PA: American Academy of Religion; distributed by Scholars Press, Missoula, MT, 1974. 210 p.

Selected papers from conferences held in 1972 and 1973, which touch on many basic issues surrounding feminist criticism of religion.

**531.** Plutarch. *Plutarch's De Iside et Osiride,* ed. with an introduction, translation, and commentary by J. Gwyn Griffiths. Aberystwyth: University of Wales, 1970. 648 p.

"On Isis and Osiris" gives one of the fuller ancient descriptions of the myths of Isis and the Mystery-rituals by which she was worshipped in Roman times. In Greek and English.

**532.** Podos, Batya. *Ariadne.* 430 Oakdale Rd., East Palo Alto, CA 94303: Frog in the Well Press, 1980. 46 p.

A powerful and moving play about Ariadne and Theseus. In this version, at the slaying of the Minotaur by Theseus the conqueror, madness drives Ariadne to the ecstatic cult of Dionysius. Nineteen pages of incidental music accompany the text.

**533.** Pomeroy, Sarah B. *Goddesses, whores, wives, and slaves: women in classical antiquity.* New York: Schocken Books, 1976. 265 p.

A classic work in women's history. In the first chapter there is some material on the Goddess but most of the book concerns women's secular lives in Greece. Pomeroy has examined a great many ancient texts, making this still one of the best sources of information on the lives of women who worshipped the Goddess.

**534.** Porterfield, Amanda. *Feminine spirituality in America: from Sarah Edwards to Martha Graham.* Philadelphia: Temple University Press, 1980. 238 p.

Of most interest is chapter 4, p. 83-98, "Witchcraft and Sexuality in Literature," which examines the motifs of sexuality and the fear of being bewitched as they were expressed in nineteenth-century American literature.

**535.** Potts, Billie. *The new woman's Tarot.* Rev. ed. Woodstock, NY: Elf and Dragon Press, 1978. 54 p.

Gives new interpretations of the cards and renames some of the figures in the Major Arcana to make them wholly woman-oriented; also gives herbal and astrological correspondences. The Tarot images themselves were not finished when the book was printed, so the illustrations are only suggestions of what was intended.

**536.** ———. *Witches heal: lesbian herbal self-sufficiency.* Bearsville, NY: Hecuba's Daughters, 1982. 172 p.

An excellent herbal that gives sensible advice and straight talk on such matters as caring for ourselves and using herbs in situations where Western medicine actually may be better for us, e.g. in abortions and in diagnostic tests. Potts writes that the traditional witch's bag of tricks, or collection of ritual tools, was the original first-aid kit. The book was published with no index, but is now being issued with a separately printed index inserted.

**537.** Pratt, Marilynn J. *God's femininity recognized: a personal religious experience.* Playa del Rey, CA: Golden Puer, 1980. 156 p.

**538.** Preller, Ludwig. *Demeter und Persephone: ein Cyclus mythologischer Untersuchungen [Demeter and Persephone: a cycle of mythological studies].* Hamburg: Perthes-Besser and Mauke, 1837. 406 p.

Describes the myths of Demeter as told by Homer and Hesiod; her relationship to Gaea, Isis, Rhea, and Hecate; the rape of Persephone; and the worship of Demeter as goddess of agriculture.

**539.** Preston, James J. *Cult of the Goddess: a social and religious change in a Hindu temple.* New Delhi: Vikas, 1980. 109 p.

On worship in the temple of the goddess Chandi in Cuttack, India.

**540.** Price, Leslie. "Witches as psychic practitioners," *Journal of Religion and Psychical Research*, 6:307–08, Oct. 1983.

**541.** Price, Theodora Hadzisteliou. *Kourotrophos: cults and representations of the Greek nursing deities.* Leiden: Brill, 1978. 240 p.

Contains a considerable amount of information on cultic practice throughout the Greek area.

**542.** Pritchard, James B. *Palestinian figurines in relation to certain goddesses known through literature.* New Haven: American Oriental Society, 1943; New York: Kraus Reprint, 1967. (PhD thesis, University of Pennsylvania, 1943) 101 p.

On the nude female figurines usually identified as those of Anath or Astarte.

**543.** Przyluski, Jean. *La grande déesse: introduction à l'étude comparative des religions [The Great Goddess: introduction to the comparative study of religion].* Paris: Payot, 1950. 204 p.

A study of the Goddess in the ancient civilizations of the Near East, Greece, and India. The work contains three parts:

"From Water- and Wood-Nymphs to the Great Goddess," which examines the evolution of the Goddess from localized deity to universal Mother; "The Avatars of the Goddess" as patron of agriculture, Triple Goddess, and Queen of Heaven; and "From the Mother Goddess to the Father God."

**544.** Purce, Jill. *The mystic spiral: journey of the soul.* New York: Thames and Hudson, 1980 (first published 1974). 128 p.

On the spiral in mythology and religion. In Goddess religion it symbolizes the rebirth of the soul.

**545.** *Quest: a feminist quarterly.* Washington DC, 1974-.

See especially vol. 1, no. 4, Spring 1975, on "Women and Spirituality," which has articles by Mary Daly, Morgan McFarland, and Sally Gearhart.

**546.** Quinn, Alice. "Eenie, meenie, miniee [sic], moe, catch a WITCH by the toe," *Majority Report,* 4(14):6, Oct. 31, 1974.

On the witch-hunts and the methods used by the authorities to extort confessions and to convict women of witchcraft.

**547.** ———. "If a woman dares to cure," *Majority Report,* 4(17):10, Dec. 15, 1974.

**548.** ———. "Witches, lesbians, mental patients," *Majority Report,* 4(12):11, Oct. 3, 1974.

**549.** Rabuzzi, Kathryn Allen. *The sacred and the feminine: towards a theology of housework.* New York: Seabury Press, 1982. 215 p.

Using Christian and Goddess imagery, Rabuzzi re-interprets the daily round of women's lives as potentially, if not actually, sacred, despite the current view of housework as meaningless and boring. She maintains that even in tedium we can find spiritual import.

**550.** Rakusin, Sudie. *Goddesses and Amazons: a journal.* N.p.: Amazon Images, 1983. 200 p.

Matriarchal artwork amid blank pages, for use as a journal.

**551.** Rapp, Rayna. "Women, religion, and archaic civilizations: an introduction," *Feminist Studies,* 4(3):1-6, Oct. 1978.

Several articles in this issue deal with woman and religion. Rapp summarizes the articles and discusses the issues raised with regard to women and religion, and religion and society.

**552.** Reed, Evelyn. *Woman's evolution: from matriarchal clan to patriarchal family.* New York: Pathfinder Press, 1975. 491 p.

A classic Marxist analysis of the shift from matrifocal to patrifocal society. Reed describes the vital but unacknowledged role played by women in the formation of society, pointing out that for most of human history we have lived in hunting-gathering societies in which women's work is economically more important than men's. By gathering food women provide up to 80% of the community's sustenance; by their knowledge of plants and as keepers of the hearth-fires, prehistoric women invented agriculture and chemistry. When the principle of paternity was discovered and private, rather than communal, ownership of property became the social norm, men began to control women so that property could be transmitted from the father to "his" offspring. Thus it is in the interests of capitalism to maintain the subordination of all producers, including the producers of life.

553. Rein, Marcy. "Off the mountains and into the streets," *Off Our Backs*, 7(6):15, July–Aug. 1977.

Rein is very critical of the women's spirituality movement, insisting that we need Marxist analysis of political questions and concrete solutions to our problems, and that a utopian philosophy alone won't get us to Utopia.

554. Remedi, Angie. *The Mother calls.* Box 67332, Los Angeles: Terra Bella Productions, 1984.

Songs of the Goddess and the seasonal festivals.

555. Renault, Mary. *The king must die.* New York: Pantheon, 1958. 338 p.

A novel of Theseus, the Minotaur, and Ariadne. Because the story is told by Theseus (and was written in the 1950's), it is rather male-oriented, but Renault's gift for understanding history as well as literature makes the ancient world and the Old Gods come alive in a way that is rarely achieved by historical novelists. Her work suggests not only what it might have been like to live in ancient Crete, but what it may have meant to serve the Mother Goddess, or Poseidon. The story of Theseus, Phaedra, and Hippolytus is continued in *The Bull from the Sea* (New York: Pantheon Books, 1962.)

556. Rich, Adrienne. "The kingdom of the fathers," *Partisan Review*, 43(1):17–37, 1976.

On the history of patriarchy and the revival of matriarchal theory in the women's movement.

557. ———. *Of woman born: motherhood as experience and institution.* New York: Norton, 1976. 318 p.

This was one of the first modern feminist works to describe not only God as Mother, but all mothers as God incarnate. Rich dissects the true meaning of matriarchy and patriarchy, examining motherhood as myth, religion, biological function, and means of oppression of women. She also considers the feminist ramifications of being the mother of sons. Her analysis opened the minds of many women in the feminist community to the ideal of a women's civilization.

**558.** Richardson, Dimitra Andriopoulos. *The Mother Goddess in Minoan Crete and vestiges in the contemporary Greek Orthodox Church.* PhD thesis, New York University, 1981. 404 p.

Richardson analyzes the role of the Goddess in Minoan Crete as described by classical authors and modern scholars. She then examines the liturgy, iconography, and festivals of the Greek Orthodox Church to locate the remnants of the Mother Goddess (as *Theotokos* or "Mother of God") and Her impact on modern Greek society. She concludes from the evidence that the Minoans valued women, nature, and sexuality, that modern Greek Christianity attempts to retain a feeling of oneness with nature by celebrating festivals associated with the Virgin Mary as Mother, and that the survival of the Goddess indicates a profound need for the presence of the Feminine in spiritual life.

**559.** Richardson, Marilyn. *Black women and religion: a bibliography.* Boston: G. K. Hall, 1980. 139 p.

An annotated list of books, articles, records and films on Afro-American women from Colonial times to the present. Most of the items deal with women and Christianity, but Richardson also includes entries on the folk traditionss of Vodun and hoodoo, a kind of folk magic practiced in the South by whites as well as blacks.

**560.** Rigney, Barbara Hill. *Lilith's daughters: women and religion in contemporary fiction.* Madison, WI: University of Wisconsin Press, 1982. 120 p.

Like Carol Christ in *Diving Deep and Surfacing*, Rigney looks at the divinity of woman as expressed in women's writing. Each chapter takes a different image: Jesus Christ (*The Dollmaker*, Harriet Arnow); Mary (*Sula*, Toni Morrison); the Garden of Eden (*The Wanderground*, Sally Gearhart; *Pilgrim at Tinker Creek*, Annie Dillard); and Eve (the works of Doris Lessing and Margaret Drabble).

**561.** Robbins, Rossell Hope. *The encyclopedia of witchcraft and demonology.* New York: Crown, 1959. 571 p.

This encyclopedia focuses exclusively on witchcraft as a Christian-defined heresy in the Burning Times of the fifteenth to eighteenth centuries. Entries are by topic (such as "Familiars"), by locality, and by the names of many individual women accused and/or convicted of witchcraft, with details of their interrogations, trials, and executions. The accounts of the horrors of the witch-hunts will make any reader's hair stand on end. Appended is a "Select Bibliography" of over 1100 books.

**562.** ———. *Witchcraft: an introduction to the literature of witchcraft; being the preface and introduction to the Catalogue of the Witchcraft Collection, Cornell University Library.* Millwood, NY: KTO Press, 1978. 121 p.
See entry 135.

**563.** Roberts, Jane. *The nature of personal reality: a Seth book.* Englewood Cliffs, NJ: Prentice-Hall, 1974. 510 p.
Roberts was an English medium who received messages and information from her spirit-guide Seth. The Seth books, particularly this work, have been very popular among spiritual feminists. Its theme that each individual can create her own reality and in fact does so all the time has been an important influence for many women in the shaping of womanspirit philosophy.

**564.** Roberts, Mark. "Effeminism, witchcraft, and Goddess worship," *Double F: A Magazine of Effeminism,* 3:26–35, Winter 1975–76. (Available at the Institute for the Study of American Religion, Box 1311, Evanston, IL 60201.)
Roberts is the partner of Morgan McFarland, feminist Dianic witch. Dianic witchcraft venerates the Mother Goddess but not the Horned God, and women take a dominant role in religious affairs. Roberts explains why he does not find this threatening.

**565.** ———. *An introduction to Dianic witchcraft.* Dallas: The Mother Grove, n.d. 71 p.

**566.** Robertson, Olivia. *The call of Isis.* Enniscorthy, Clonegal, Eire: Cesara Publications, 1975. 126 p.
Robertson and her brother, Lord Durdin-Robertson, have founded the Fellowship of Isis, a kind of non-sectarian Goddess religion that is influenced by ritual magic.

**567.** ———. *Dea: rites and mysteries of the Goddess; liturgy of the Fellowship of Isis.* Dublin: DOFAS, 1985. 55 p.

**568.** ———. *The Isis wedding rite.* Enniscorthy, Clonegal, Eire: Cesara Publications, 1975. 16 p.

**569.** ———. *Ordination of a priestess.* Enniscorthy, Clonegal, Eire: Cesara Publications, 1977. 16 p.

**570.** ———. *Rite of rebirth: initiation of the Fellowship of Isis.* Enniscorthy, Clonegal, Eire: Cesara Publications, 1975. 20 p.

**571.** ———. *Urania: ceremonial magic of the Goddess.* Enniscorthy, Clonegal, Eire: Cesara Publications, n.d. 66 p.
Liturgy of the Fellowship of Isis: a collection of rituals dedicated to the cosmic and planetary forces. Each ritual centers on a different goddess, among them the Morrigan of

Ireland, Sarasvati, the African moon goddess Ngame, Kundalini, Astarte, Inanna, and Hathor.

572. ———, and Lord Strathloch, eds. *The Fellowship of Isis directory for 1980.* Enniscorthy, Clonegal, Eire: Cesara Publications, 1979. 52 p.

573. Roden, Lois I. *In Her image.* Waco, TX: Living Waters, 1981. 34 p.
On the femininity of God.

574. Rohrlich, Ruby. "State formation in Sumer and the subjugation of women," *Feminist Studies,* 6(1):76-102, 1980.
Rohrlich is an anthropologist who has investigated the transition from peaceful, matrifocal, Goddess-centered Neolithic communities such as Çatal Hüyük—which, she points out, is generally neglected in history and anthropology texts—to the Mesopotamian patriarchal city-state, which is characterized by commerce, social stratification, oppression, and imperialism. She outlines the shift in early Sumer from queens, goddesses, and priestesses to kings, gods, priests, male officials and landowners, slavery, and secular prostitution.

575. ———. "Women in transition: Crete and Sumer," in *Becoming visible: women in European history,* ed. Renate Bridenthal and Claudia Koontz. Boston: Houghton Mifflin, 1977.
A study of the development of civilization and the patriarchal state and the impact this had on women's lives. Rohrlich gives a sketch of Cretan society and women's place in it and describes the transition from Neolithic culture to urban civilization in Sumer. Another article by this title, which is an amalgamation of the two articles cited here, appears in *Women in Search of Utopia: Mavericks and Mythmakers,* edited with introductions by Rohrlich and Elaine Hoffman Baruch. New York: Schocken Books, 1984, p. 30-42.)

576. Romero, Joan Arnold, comp. *Women and religion, 1973: preprinted papers for the Working Group on Women and Religion,* Judith Plaskow Goldenberg and Joan Arnold Romero, cochairpersons. Tallahassee: American Academy of Religion, 1973. 127 p.
Papers written for the annual meeting of the AAR, Chicago, November 1973.

577. Rose. "Spirituality: witches," *Big Mama Rag,* 10(3):16, March 1982.

578. Rose, Elliot. *A razor for a goat: a discussion of certain problems in the history of witchcraft and diabolism.* Toronto: University of Toronto Press, 1962. 257 p.

A thorough treatment of the phenomenon of European witchcraft with special regard to Murray's theories. Rose is careful to distinguish between folk survivals *from* paganism and folk survivals *of* paganism. This work contains a great deal of interesting information, and Rose's theories may be as controversial as Murray's.

**579.** Rose, Jeanne. *Herbs and things: Jeanne Rose's herbal.* New York: Grosset and Dunlap, 1972. 323 p.

One of the best modern herbals available. Gives a listing of many herbs and plant substances with their uses, a glossary, and several well-organized chapters on ailments with recipes for home remedies and cosmetics. There is also a chapter on the magical and psychic uses of herbs, listing many old formulas. By now some of Rose's opinions on dieting, drugs, and douches will seem very outdated, but for comprehensiveness of coverage, organization, and specificity of instructions, this is still one of the most useful herbals around.

**580.** Ross, Anne. *Pagan Celtic Britain: studies in iconography and tradition.* New York: Columbia University Press, 1967. 433 p.

The most complete treatment at this time of Celtic religion and its many cultic features. Contains a separate chapter on the Goddess as divine hag, as horse, as mother, as sheela-na-gig, and her association with wells and rivers in the Celtic world.

**581.** Rothery, Guy Cadogan. *The Amazons in antiquity and modern times.* London: F. Griffiths, 1910; also in the Gerritsen Women's History Microfilm Series, no. 2444. 218 p.

The first part deals with Classical Amazons; the second with "Amazons" of modern times.

**582.** Ruether, Rosemary Radford. "Goddesses and witches: liberation and counter cultural feminism," *Christian Century*, 97(28): 824–47, Sept. 10–17, 1980.

Ruether, a Protestant theologian, is one of the most prolific writers in the women's spirituality movement. Listed below are those works that are most relevant to woman-centered spirituality; she has authored or edited several others on women in Judeo-Christian religion. An ardent supporter of the feminist religious revival, she nevertheless does not tolerate fuzzy thinking from any quarter. In this article she criticizes Feminist Wicca and the thought of Carol Christ and Naomi Goldenberg for its lack of historical accuracy and for assumptions they make about sexual politics. She implies that feminist Goddess religion has fascistic elements in its rejection of Western civilization and its extolling of nature.

583. ———. *Mary, the feminine face of the Church.* Philadelphia: Westminster Press, 1977. 106 p.

A guide for study groups in Protestant denominations, which have long neglected or suppressed veneration of the Virgin. Ruether describes Mary's relationship to other Near Eastern images of the Feminine Divine and to the Biblical feminine imagery of God. She seeks to re-affirm the spiritual importance of the Feminine as embodied in the Virgin, and advocates a re-assessment of Mary in order to help rid Christianity of the arid masculinity that has too often characterized Protestant thought.

584. ———. *New woman/new earth: sexist ideologies and human liberation.* New York: Seabury Press, 1975. 221 p.

Includes chapters on witches and Jews as the Other in Christian history, and on Mary as Queen of Heaven. In the second part of the book Ruether looks at liberation theology: she stresses that sexism is an integral part of all oppressive social systems and warns that no liberation movement can afford to ignore women.

585. ———. "The persecution of witches: a case of sexism and agism?" *Christianity and Crisis*, 34(22):291-95, Dec. 23, 1974.

In this article Ruether points out that the witch-hunts were often largely directed against older women.

586. ———. *The religious sacralization of patriarchy.* Rochester, NY: Women's Ordination Conference, 1983. 13 p.

587. ———. *Sexism and God-talk: towards a feminist theology.* Boston: Beacon Press, 1983. 289 p.

In this work Ruether attempts to truly integrate feminist thought with traditional theology. It is her belief that Christianity is powerful enough to accord women the spiritual dignity we deserve, but she is not afraid to ask tough questions of her religion, e.g. can a male savior have any real meaning for women? This work covers many other important issues, such as the sexism of using the male gender to refer to God, the concept of woman=body=nature, and the hope of socio-economic liberation through feminism.

588. ———. "The way of Wicca," *Christian Century*, 97(6):208-09, Feb. 20, 1980.

A review of Starhawk's *The Spiral Dance*. Ruether is sympathetic to the Goddess movement but has a few criticisms and challenges to spiritual feminists, which, though they come from a Judeo-Christian context, are thought-provoking: what is the origin of evil? How did we fall from the Golden Age?

589. ———. "Woman, ecology, and the domination of nature," *Ecumenist,* 14(1):1-5, Nov.-Dec. 1975.

On the oppression of woman in nature and in religion, and how this has been fostered by patriarchy and has supported male domination.

5'90. ———, ed. *Womanguides: texts for doing feminist theology.* Boston: Beacon Press, 1985. 274 p.

An anthology of woman-centered texts taken from ancient Goddess religions, the Old and New Testaments, and recent feminist writing, designed to be used in courses on women's spirituality. The material is arranged by topic, such as gender imagery of God, creation stories, the saviour/redemptrix figure, and visions of a new society. Each chapter contains selections from several different historical periods.

591. Runeberg, Arne. *Witches, demons, and fertility magic: analysis of their significance and mutual relations in West-European folk religion.* Thesis, Helsinki, 1947 (Finska Vetenskaps-Societeten. Commentationes humanarum letterarum, XIV, 4); Norwood, PA: Norwood Editions, 1979. 273 p.

Examines witchcraft as fertility religion and magical system, the development of European witchcraft, folk beliefs, and the Sabbats as seasonal festivals.

592. Rush, Anne Kent. *Moon, moon.* Berkeley: Moon Books, 1976. 415 p.

A delightful compendium of moon-lore, beginning with the science of selenology and an interview with an astronaut. Rush provides a fountain of information about moon goddesses and moon rituals from many cultures, including African, Native American, Australian, and Polynesian; a lunar calendar; the moon's effect on the body, plants, and animals; feminist rituals, chants, songs, poetry, folklore, and artwork. Some of the contributors are Mary Daly, Monique Wittig, Hallie Iglehart, and Z Budapest. A joyous visit with the Goddess.

593. Russell, Jeffrey Burton. *A history of witchcraft: sorcerers, heretics, and pagans.* London: Thames and Hudson, 1980. 192 p.

A general history that covers all aspects of witchcraft, from indigenous magical traditions to Western European witchcraft and feminist Wicca. There are several sections on women as witches, past and present, and many illustrations. Russell believes that what was called "witchcraft" by the authorities of Church and State actually was a variety of religious movements that ran the gamut from pre-Christian magic to heresies such as Catharism.

594. ———. *Witchcraft in the Middle Ages.* Ithaca: Cornell University Press, 1972. 394 p.

A classic historical work. Although many writers speak of "the mediaeval witch-hunts," the persecution of witches did not peak until the Renaissance and early modern period, i.e. the sixteenth and seventeenth centuries. Russell's work, however, deals exclusively with the centuries before the publication of *Malleus Maleficarum* by Heinrich Kramer and Jakob Sprenger in 1487. He believes that the witch-hunts were intended to be the culmination—the final solution—of the long battle between Christianity and paganism. While he recognizes witchcraft as a form of social and religious dissent he does not claim that it was in fact an organized pagan religion.

595. Salmonson, Jessica Amanda, ed. *Amazons!* New York: Daw, 1979. 206 p.

596. ———., ed. *Amazons II.* New York: Daw, 1981. 239 p.
   Two collections of stories about warrior women that range from Classical settings to sword-and-sorcery to contemporary fiction. Most of the authors are women.

597. Samuel, Pierre. *Amazones, guerrières et gaillardes [Amazons, warriors and wenches].* Brussels: Editions Complexe; Grenoble: Presses Universitaires de Grenoble, 1975. 315 p.
   Introduction by Françoise d'Eaubonne.

598. Sangren, P. Steven. "Female gender in Chinese religious symbols: Kuan Yin, Ma Tsu, and the Eternal Mother," *Signs,* 9:4-25, Autumn 1983.
   Like Kuan Yin, Ma Tsu is a benevolent protectress; the Eternal Mother is the supreme deity of several Taiwanese sects.

599. Schafer, Edward H. *The divine woman: dragon ladies and rain maidens.* Berkeley: University of California Press, 1973; San Francisco: North Point Press, 1980. 239 p.
   On the Goddess in T'ang literature. Many Chinese goddesses were associated with water as divinities of the sea, rivers, lakes, and especially rain, the most important of these goddesses being Nu Kua. They were also associated with the dragon, which in Chinese folklore is a beneficent creature thought to bring rain. Much of the poetry referring to Chinese water goddesses was composed by male and female shamans (Schafer uses the Russian word "shamanka" to refer to female shamans).

600. Schaupp, Joan. *Woman: image of the Holy Spirit.* Denville, NJ: Dimension Books, 1975. 124 p.
   The Holy Spirit is usually spoken of as male, yet in Hebrew "spirit" (*ruach*) is a feminine noun; in Biblical Greek it is neuter (*pneuma*). In the early days of the Church there was a

movement to make the Holy Spirit female which was quickly suppressed by the Church fathers. Some feminist Christians are now trying to revive this image.

601. Schilling, Silke. *Die Schlangenfrau: über matriarchale Symbolik weiblicher Identität und ihre Aufhebung in Mythologie, Märchen, Sage, und Literatur [The snake-woman: on the matriarchal symbolism of female identity, and its suppression in mythology, fairy tales, sagas, and literature].* Frankfurt: Materialis, 1984. 331 p.

Schilling examines the folklore and mythology of the relationship between women and snakes. She observes that in Goddess religions the snake was a sacred animal, yet in the epic literature of the early patriarchal age—in Scandinavia, Greece, and Babylon, among other cultures—male warriors are praised for defeating serpents and dragons: for example, the water goddess Tiamat becomes a sea-demon to the Babylonians. Ironically, over time the snake gradually became associated with the male principle of sexuality and death rather than with the female's powers of regeneration.

602. *Schlangenbrut.* c/o Gabrielle Gummel, Giselbertstrasse 24, 5060 Ber-Gladsach 1, West Germany, 1984-.

A German periodical devoted to feminist spirituality.

603. Schneider, Monique. *De l'exorcisme à la psychanalyse: le feminin expurgé [From exorcism to psychoanalysis: the Feminine expurgated].* Paris: Retz, 1979. 189 p.

On mediaeval exorcism of demons, the witch-hunts, and modern Freudian psychoanalysis as examples of the war against women.

604. Schreier, Josefine. *Göttinnen: ihr Einfluss von der Urzeit bis zur Gegenwart [Goddesses: their influence from prehistory to the present].* Vienna: Rohrer, 1968; Munich: Frauenoffensive, 1978. 181 p.

Contains many illustrations of the Goddess.

605. Schultz, Ted. "Busting fortune tellers: a modern persecution," *Co-evolution Quarterly,* no. 42, p. 52–58, Summer 1984.

On the current legal and judicial state of affairs regarding fortune-telling, and the history of persecution and prosecution of fortune-tellers. Anyone who performs divination for money should read this.

606. Seljan, Zora A. O. *Iemanjá e suas lendas [Iemanjá and her legends].* Rio de Janeiro: Grafica Record Editôra, 1967. 210 p.

607. ———. *Iemanjá, mãe dos orixás [Iemanjá, mother of the orixás].* Preface by Jorge Amado. São Paulo: Editôra Afro-Brasileira, 1973. 179 p.

The *orixás* are the gods or spirits of Umbanda, the Brazilian descendant of the religion of the West African Yoruba people. Umbanda came to Brazil with slavery and is now so deeply ingrained in the national culture that during the planning of Brasilia plots of land were set aside for *terreros,* or houses of Umbanda, just as they were reserved for churches and schools. Iemanjá, a goddess of the sea and the moon, is the most important female deity in Umbanda. She is often depicted as a mermaid in her "Water Mother" aspect. Both of Seljan's books give legends and stories of Iemanjá's intercession.

608. Sen, Sukumar. *The Great Goddesses in Indic tradition.* Calcutta: Papyrus, 1983. 74 p.

609. Shange, Ntozake. *Sassafrass, Cypress, and Indigo: a novel.* New York: St. Martin's Press, 1982. 224 p.

A beautiful story of three sisters growing up in the South; Sassafrass, a weaver, and Cypress, a dancer, leave the South to create their own lives, while Indigo stays, pursuing the ancient ways of Black women by studying ritual and healing. You won't find many novels that include meditations, rituals, and recipes.

610. Sharon Rose. "Is God a male chauvinist?" *Off Our Backs* 1(21):6, May 6, 1971.

On the conflict between traditional Judaism and feminism. (This issue of *OOB* is devoted to Jewish women.)

611. Lady Sheba. *The grimoire of Lady Sheba.* 2nd ed. St. Paul: Llewellyn Publications, 1974 (first published as *Lady Sheba's Book of Shadows,* 1971). 236 p.

A Book of Shadows from the Gardnerian tradition of witchcraft, one of the first manuals published in modern times. Contains a great deal of useful information, e.g. Craft laws, witch language, rituals, dances. Some practices, however, are not at all feminist—e.g. since the High Priestess represents the Goddess, she must be young and beautiful, and when she is no longer young she must turn her office over to a younger woman.

612. *Shekhinah Magazine.* Box 4098, Waco, TX 76705. Dec. 1980-.

A quarterly edited by Lois I. Roden (see entry 573) that seeks to explore the femininity of the Holy Spirit. Contributions are by Jews as well as Christians.

613. Sheridan, Ronald, and Anne Ross. *Gargoyles and grotesques: paganism in the medieval church.* Boston: New York Graphic Society, 1975. 127 p.

Medieval churches contained many hidden (and overt) representations of the pagan Celtic deities in the form of the

Green Man (a version of the pagan god) and the sheela-na-gig, a frankly sexual female figure. The authors observe that as there are no contemporary mediaeval writings that describe or explain the pagan symbols (for obvious reasons), modern interpretations must remain open to question.

614. Shields, Emily Ledyard. *Juno: a study in early Roman religion.* Northampton, MA: Smith College, 1926. 74 p.

An interesting study of Juno's pre-patriarchal origins and her relationship to the moon and to other deities, e.g. Lucina, Janus, Hercules.

615. Shinn, Larry. "The Goddess: theological sign or religious symbol?" *Numen,* 31(2):175–98, Dec. 1984.

A historian of religion examines feminist spirituality as a religious phenomenon in its own right. Shinn points out that feminists tend to regard the Goddess as a symbol rather than an actual entity. In a similar vein he analyzes the image of the goddess Kali as a symbol for Hindus.

616. Showerman, Grant. *The Great Mother of the Gods.* Madison, WI: University of Wisconsin, 1901; Chicago: Argonaut, 1969. (PhD thesis, University of Wisconsin; Bulletin of the University of Wisconsin, no. 43) 113 p.

On the goddess Cybele from her Anatolian origins to her important Roman cult.

617. Shuttle, Penelope, and Peter Redgrove. *The wise wound: Eve's curse and Everywoman.* New York: R. Marek, 1978. 335 p.

A book for the general reader on the folklore of menstruation. The authors begin with scientific knowledge about menstruation, stressing that much is still not yet understood or is misunderstood. They then describe the ways in which societies past and present have regarded the menstruating woman, the mystical and actual effects of the moon on menstruation, and the relationship of menstruation to moon-religions and ancient blood rites. The witch-hunts are interpreted as a reflection of a very primitive fear and loathing of women. The authors conclude with a plea for us to see menstruation not as a curse but as a mark of the Divine.

618. Shwartz, Susan M., ed. *Hecate's cauldron.* New York: Daw, 1982. 256 p.

Thirteen fantasy/sword-and-sorcery stories, all but two by women, with a common theme of witchcraft and magic. Most have positive images of the witch, and several are influenced by feminist spirituality. The authors include Andre Norton, Tanith Lee, Jessica Salmonson, and C. J. Cherryh. Includes a bibliography of relevant fiction and non-fiction.

**619.** Sierksma, Fokke. *Religie, sexualiteit en agressie: een cultuur-psychologische bijdrage tot de verklaring van de spanning tussen de sexen [Religion, sexuality, and aggression: a cultural and psychological contribution towards explaining tension between the sexes].* Groningen: Konstapel, 1979. 341 p.
On the matriarchal mythos and the origins of sex roles.

**620.** Singer, June K. *Androgyny: toward a new theory of sexuality.* Garden City: Anchor Press, 1976. 371 p.
Androgyny as a liberating ideal discussed from a psycho-analytical perspective, with reference to its treatment in many cultures and philosophical systems, from the matriarchal age to the Kabbalah and Eastern thought.

**621.** Sirius, Jean. *And every one of us a witch.* Brooklyn, NY: Sirius Books, 1979. (First edition published as *Womyn/Friends* in 1978) 22 p.
Feminist poems; drawings by Billie Potts.

**623.** ———. *The green womon poems*; drawings by Gaia. Box 1027, Brooklyn, NY: Sirius Books, 1980. 25 p.
A little book about wise women, witches, and lesbians.

**624.** *Sister Heathenspinster's lunation calendar.* 809 Haggard St., Iowa City, IA 52240. 1976—
A lunar calendar that begins at the Spring Equinox. Like Passmore's calendar, the days are arranged in spirals rather than in straght lines.

**625.** Sjöö, Monica. *The ancient religion of the Great Cosmic Mother of all*; edited and extended by Barbara Mor. Trondheim, Norway: Rainbow Press, 1981. 80 p.
Sjöö, a Swedish-born artist living in England, recognized women's divine power and creativity some twenty years ago. She began researching Goddess culture and matriarchy, finding more and more evidence of the suppression of women's power by patriarchal religions and social systems. Here she writes on the Goddess, ancient matriarchies, witches, the sacredness of women's blood, and the Goddess in Britain and Malta. Illustrated with many examples of her pioneering matriarchal artwork.

**626.** ———. "In defence of feminism," *Peace News*, Nottingham, Eng., 20(70):12, May 19, 1978.

**627.** Slater, Philip E. *The glory of Hera: Greek mythology and the Greek family.* Boston: Beacon Press, 1968. 513 p.
A psychoanalytical study of the Greek family and intersexual relations. The central portion is on "Mythical Defenses against the Maternal Threat," as reflected in the patriarchal mythos of Zeus, Dionysius, et al.

**628.** Smyth, Frank. *Modern witchcraft: the fascinating study of the rebirth of paganism and magic.* New York: Harper and Row, 1973 (first published in London, 1970). 127 p.

Smyth describes traditional European witchcraft and the witch-hunts, witchcraft in the U.S., and the revival of the Craft in Britain under the leadership of Gerald Gardner and others. He emphasizes the Goddess and nature religion.

**629.** Snyder-Ott, Joelynn. *Women and creativity.* Millbrae, CA: Les Femmes Publishing, 1978. 144 p.

An artist examines women's art and feminine ways of interpreting reality. See especially the chapter on "Female Iconography at Stonehenge," which the author and her daughter recognized as a woman's place, the spaces between the upright stones reminding them of birth-passages.

**630.** Sobol, Donald J. *The Amazons of Greek mythology.* South Brunswick, NJ: A. S. Barnes, 1972. 174 p.

One of the most thorough treatments of Amazons in the ancient world. Sobol gives a great deal of detailed information on the Amazons of Libya, Asia Minor, and Scythia; however, some readers may find his tone condescending and offensive.

**631.** Solmsen, Friedrich. *Isis among the Greeks and Romans.* Cambridge, MA: published for Oberlin College by Harvard University Press, 1979. (Martin Classical lectures, v. 25) 156 p.

A brief study of the worship of Isis as it persisted after the fall of Egypt to the Greeks.

**632.** Somer, Carol. "How women had control of their lives and lost it," *Second Wave,* 2(3):5–10, 28, Fall 1972.

A well-documented history of male control over women's health, with a section on the midwife as witch.

*633.* ———. "Witches, hurricanes, other feminists," *Second Wave,* 1(1):31, Spring 1971.

**634.** *Songs for the Old Religion.* 2nd ed. Oakland, CA: Nemeton, 1973. 26 p.

A songbook for Neo-Pagans.

**635.** Spretnak, Charlene. *Lost goddesses of early Greece: a collection of pre-Hellenic myths.* Berkeley: Moon Books, 1978; new edition: Boston: Beacon Press, 1984. 132 p.

When Spretnak wanted to introduce her daughter to the Greek myths, she realized that most versions portray women as either helpless (the numerous raped nymphs) or evil (Pandora, jealous Hera). Not wishing to teach her daughter self-hatred, and having learned from other feminists that a goddess-centered era had preceded the formation of the androcentric versions of the Olympian myths, she set about researching and re-writing the stories of the Greek goddesses, attempting to recapture their original woman-centered flavor. Her versions provide non-sexist myths for children. The first edition has lovely original illustrations by Edidt Geever; the second uses images of the Great Goddess taken from Cretan seals.

**636.** ———, ed. *The politics of women's spirituality: essays on the rise of spiritual power within the feminist movement.* Garden City: Anchor Books, 1982. 590 p.

This is one of the most important books to have arisen from the women's spirituality movement. If only one book is to be read on the subject, it should be this collection. Many of the most prominent authors are represented, including Starhawk, Marija Gimbutas, Carol Christ, Merlin Stone, Sally Gearhart. In addition to the better-known feminist authors, feminist spirituality is discussed by Black, Asian, and Native American women. Also of interest are articles on the applications of feminist spirituality to political action in rape crisis centers, in the ecology movement, peace activism, and reproductive rights. There is also a section on the new "holy war" being waged by the religious Right against feminism and women's freedoms, and an extensive bibliography on women's spirituality, especially in its political context.

**637.** Srivastava, Mahesh C. P. *Mother goddesses in Indian art, archaeology, and literature.* Delhi: Agam Kala Prakashan, 1977. 231 p.

An excellent resource for the study of the Indian goddess. The author traces the Indian Mother Goddess from Neolithic times to the present, drawing parallels between the Venus figures found in Paleolithic and Neolithic Europe and female figurines found in the Indus Valley civilizations of some 5000 years ago. In the Vedic period, which began with the Indo-European invasions of the second millennium B.C., male deities were supreme but the familiar Hindu goddesses began to appear; the Gupta period, from the third century A.D., produced many sacred and literary texts in which goddesses or other female figures are important. The author also discusses Tantric Buddhism and contemporary festivals dedicated to Kali, Sarasvati, and other goddesses.

**638.** Starhawk. *Dreaming the dark: magic, sex, and politics.* Boston: Beacon Press, 1982. 242 p.

Starhawk is a witch and practicing psychotherapist who has been one of the foremost spokeswomen for feminist spirituality and feminist witchcraft. Since the publication of

*The Spiral Dance* she has devoted more of her attention to political activism against the military and nuclear power. In this book she expands her Goddess thealogy, interpreting socioeconomic issues such as poverty, ecology, and political power in the light of New Age philosophy. The feminist/New Age definition of power is that power is not a scarce commodity that is diminished when shared; rather, power, and by extension, divinity, is immanent: it comes from within ourselves instead of being imposed on us or others from without. To experience this new interpretation of power Starhawk gives exercises for use in political action groups. Much of the text describes how she has applied her religion and use of magic to political action and in empowerment groups. Appended is an insightful explanation of the origins of the witch-hunts, which she correlates with the rise during the Renaissance of a professional, educated, male elite.

**639.** ———. "The Goddess of Witchcraft," *Anima,* 5(2): 125–29, Spring 1979.

Excerpted in part from *The Spiral Dance,* this article describes the Goddess as the creative life-force that underlies all things in the universe.

**640.** ———. *The spiral dance: a rebirth of the ancient religion of the Great Goddess.* San Francisco: Harper and Row, 1978. 218 p.

One of the most influential works of women's spirituality. Starhawk gives an explanation of witchcraft that is rooted in contemporary psychology and feminism; her gift is that she is able to explain to the intelligent reader a subject with controversial associations in a non-threatening and non-sensational way. She is the closest that feminist witchcraft has to a thealogian, although she herself rejects this role. Her thealogy views the Craft concept of magic as nothing less than applied physics, and presents the Goddess and pagan God as liberating symbols for women and men. Readers interested in men's liberation will find the chapter on the male deity quite valuable. This book gives many exercises and examples of rituals and spells, and is probably the most widely used manual among spiritual feminists.

**641.** Starrett, Barbara. *I dream in female: the metaphors of evolution and the metaphors of power.* Box 1516, Vineyard Haven, MA 02568: Cassandra Press, 1977; also printed in *The Lesbian Reader,* ed. Gina Covina and Laurel Galana. Berkeley: Amazon Press, 1975, p. 105–21.

One of the earliest works on the dualistic, restrictive philosophy of patriarchy and the liberating, holistic possibilities of feminist thought.

**642.** Stein, Diane. *The Kwan Yin Book of Changes.* St. Paul: Llewellyn Publications, 1985.

Many feminists have been using the *I Ching* as a meditative aid to decision-making, yet have not felt comfortable with its patriarchal and classist biases. Stein has finally provided us with a matriarchal version that uses the symbols of wood, water, fire, mountain, etc., couched in feminine imagery, presenting the readings not as fatalistic pronouncements but as tools for growth and personal choice.

**643.** Stokley, Nancy. "Witches are sisters, too," *Women's Press,* 3(6):1, Sept. 1973.

On witchcraft as pre-Christian paganism and the witch-hunts as the political oppression of women.

**644.** Stone, Merlin. *Ancient mirrors of womanhood: our Goddess and heroine heritage.* New York: New Sibylline Press, 1979–80, 2 vols.; 1 vol. ed.: Boston: Beacon Press, 1984. 425 p.

A loving collection of myths and stories of goddesses from every major cultural grouping and continent—Celtic, Germanic and Norse, Greek, Egyptian, Mesopotamian, African, Indian, Chinese, Japanese, Native American, Australian, and Pacific—illustrated by the author's daughter.

**645.** ———. "Spirituality: a third view," *Off Our Backs,* 7(9):17, Nov. 1977.

A long letter written in defense of the feminist spirituality movement in which Stone denounces religious sexism, racism, and homophobia.

**646.** ———. *When God was a woman.* New York: Dial Press, 1976; first published in Britain as *The Paradise Papers.* 265 p.

An excellent description of the transition from matriarchal to patriarchal religion in the civilizations of the Eastern Mediterranean and the subsequent degraded position of the female. Chronologies are provided for the major civilizations, as well as an extensive bibliography on ancient religion. Considering that Stone was breaking new ground with her Goddess-centered historical research, the occasional factual error or wild speculation may be forgiven. Required reading for anyone investigating ancient Goddess religion.

**647.** Stoye, Mark. *Evolution of the worship of the Goddess in ancient Indian religions, c. 3000 B.C. to 1000 A.D.* MA thesis, Graduate Theological Union, 1979. 92 p.

**648.** Suhr, Elmer. *The spinning Aphrodite: the evolution of the Goddess from the earliest pre-Hellenic symbolism through late Classical times.* New York: Helios Books, 1969. 218 p.

On spinning, an almost universally female task, and its portrayal in Greek art as a symbol of the spiral of fate. Aphrodite, usually thought of as the goddess of beauty and heterosexuality, is frequently depicted as spinning. Suhr identifies her with the Three Fates, especially Clotho, who spins the thread of life. This is an unusual look at a goddess whom feminists often feel uncomfortable with.

**649.** Swidler, Arlene, ed. *Sistercelebrations: nine worship experiences.* Philadelphia: Fortress Press, 1974. 88 p.

Christian liturgies celebrating woman-centered holidays and rites, such as a liturgy for Mother's Day, "Brit Kedusha: a home ceremony celebrating the birth of a daughter," a mass for Women's Equality Day, a ritual to memorialize the witches, and a women's Haggadah.

**650.** "A Symposium on spiritual politics," *Co-evolution Quarterly*, no. 39, p. 26-35, Fall 1983.

A collection of short articles by a variety of spiritual and political activists, including Susan Griffin, "Entering very dangerous territory,", p. 27-28, and Starhawk, "A set of values, not beliefs," p. 30-32.

**651.** Teish, Luisah. *Jambalaya: the natural woman's book of personal charms and practical rituals.* San Francisco: Harper and Row, 1985. 268 p.

A truly groundbreaking book for Black feminist spirituality. The author tells of her own journey back to her African roots via the Black folk religion of Vodun, to which she was exposed as a child growing up in New Orleans. Teish is now a priestess in the Yoruban religion and has made her faith a blend of African religion and Vodun. She gives spells, rituals, and purification ceremonies; describes the use of candles, oils, and incense; the construction of altars; and ways to know the goddesses and gods of Africa. She presents a woman-centered feminist spirituality for Black women, but other women can also learn a great deal from her.

**652.** Teubal, Savina J. *Sarah the priestess: the first matriarch of Genesis.* Athens, Ohio: Swallow Press, 1984. 199 p.

On Sarah, wife of Abraham, as divine consort and as priestess. Teubal sees Sarah as an image of matriarchy struggling against the rising tide of patriarchy. From her story we can learn about the survival of matriarchal power in Old Testament times and the pre-patriarchal social system still evident in Genesis (matrilocal marriage, matrilineal descent).

**653.** *Thesmophoria.* Oakland, CA, 1978-. (Published 1978-81 as *Themis.*)

A short newsletter edited by Z Budapest and friends, containing brief articles, poetry, and book reviews. Published at the Sabbats.

654. Thiébaux, Marcelle. "A mythology for women: Monique Wittig's *Les Guerillères,*" *13th Moon,* 4(1):37–45, 1978.

A critical review of Wittig's epic of feminist liberation. Thiébaux describes how Wittig re-shapes language, mythology, and history to reflect a woman's way of seeing. In all of her works Wittig has redefined words, their usage, and the practice of literature itself.

655. Thompson, Louise. "Modern witches meet on Staten Island," *Majority Report,* 6(14):9, Nov. 13, 1976.

A report on the "Celebration of the Beguines" conference on women's spirituality held at Staten Island Community College, Oct. 30–31, 1976. Thompson is very critical of the workshops and the politics of the participants.

656. Thorsten, Geraldine. *God herself: the feminine roots of astrology.* New York: Avon, 1980. 414 p.

Thorsten uses goddess and Amazon images in place of the customary astrological symbols while retaining most of the traditional interpretations and connotations of each sign—e.g. the emblem of Saggitarius is the Amazon, that of Pisces is Kuan Yin. Each sign is analyzed from a feminist, matriarchal perspective. The chapter on each sign is preceded by an essay on the particular goddess or mythic figure and her worship in history. Thorsten also discusses the pre-patriarchal origins of astrology, pointing out that, due to the precession of the equinoxes, the zodiac began with Taurus in the matriarchal age (ca. 5000 to 2500 B.C.), during the time that cow and bull worship was most pervasive in Crete and the Near East.

657. Tiffany, Sharon W. "The power of matriarchal ideas," *International Journal of Women's Studies,* 5(2):138–47, 1982.

An anthropologist discusses the effect the concept of matriarchy has had on feminism and on the discipline of anthropology.

658. Tindall, Gillian. *A handbook on witches.* New York: Atheneum, 1965. 155 p.

A general work on European witchcraft, with a discussion of Margaret Murray's theory of witchcraft as an ancient fertility religion, and an interview with a British witch. I include this work for personal reasons: it taught me, in 1968, that witches were real and not a figment of the Inquisitors' imaginations, and gave me an entirely new perspective on magic.

**659.** Tiwari, Jagdish N. *Studies in Goddess cults in northern India: with special reference to the first seven centuries A.D.* PhD thesis, Australian National University, 1971. 358 p.

**660.** "Today's Joans of Arc: ritual," *Majority Report*, 4(12):6, Oct. 31, 1974.

**661.** Tran-Tam-Tinh, V., and Yvette Labrecque. *Isis lactans: corpus des monuments greco-romains d'Isis allaitant Harpocrate [Nursing Isis: corpus of Greco-Roman monuments of Isis nursing Harpocrates].* Leiden: Brill, 1973. (Etudes preliminaires aux religions orientales dans l'Empire Romain, v. 37) 225 p., 78 plates.

A catalogue of depictions of the Goddess nursing, from Egyptian times (as Isis) to mediaeval times (as Mary).

**662.** Travers, P. L., and Michael Dames. "If she's not gone, she lives there still," *Parabola*, 3(1):78–91, 1978.

A conversation on the image of the Great Goddess in Silbury Hill, England.

**663.** Trevor-Roper, Hugh R. *The European witch-craze of the sixteenth and seventeenth centuries, and other essays.* New York: Harper and Row, 1969. 246 p. (Also appears as a chapter in his *The Crisis of the Seventeenth Century*, New York: Harper and Row, 1968, p. 90–192.)

A classic analysis of the witch-hunts as a form of social control exerted by a dying ruling class and a rising middle class.

**664.** Tyrrell, William B. *Amazons: a study in Athenian mythmaking.* Baltimore: The Johns Hopkins University Press, 1984. 166 p.

Describes Amazons in the myths of Hercules and Theseus, the issue of the historicity of an Amazon nation and/or matriarchy, marriage as a way of maintaining social order in ancient Greece, and the character of Clytemnestra—whom the author regards as a kind of Amazon, with her dominant personality and rejection of the strictures of marriage. Tyrrell is less concerned with whether the Amazons ever actually existed than with the way Greek socio-sexual ideals were expressed in the myths about them. In essence, he says, Greek men viewed the Amazon as the epitome of the woman outside of marriage—a threat to patriarchal social order.

**665.** Ulanov, Ann Belford. *The Feminine in Jungian psychology and in Christian theology.* Evanston, IL: Northwestern University Press, 1971. 347 p.

An early attempt to re-integrate the Feminine into our concept of the numinous. Ulanov first describes Jungian theories on the feminine, the psyche, and the psyche in religious thought, and then discusses the psychology of women, archetypes, the anima and animus. In her discussion of the Feminine in Christian thought she emphasizes the redemptive power of love and points out the necessity for religious thinkers to learn to cultivate the Feminine and the relational mode of thought.

**666.** U.S. April 9th Collective. "Excerpts from a woman's Seder," *Off Our Backs*, 1(21):6, May 6, 1971.

A celebration of Passover as a woman's release from the bondage of men.

**667.** Valiente, Doreen. *An ABC of Witchcraft, past and present.* New York: St. Martin's Press, 1974. 377 p.

An informative dictionary of witchcraft by an English witch. She covers such topics as witches' alphabets, Druids, magical tools, and megaliths.

**668.** ———. *Natural magic.* New York: St. Martin's Press, 1975. 184 p.

A handbook on the use of nature—animals, plants, and the weather—in the occult and in ritual. Valiente provides a number of magical rites to perform for the benefit of the reader's garden.

**669.** ———. *Witchcraft for tomorrow.* New York: St. Martin's Press, 1978; London: Robert Hale, 1983. 205 p.

An overview of present trends in witchcraft and a useful companion to the other manuals listed in this bibliography. The author describes Pagan deities and the festivals, tools, practices and philosophy of the Craft. Appended is a Book of Shadows which gives directions on casting the ritual circle, the organization of the coven, chants, moon rituals, etc.

**670.** Van Vuuren, Nancy. *The subversion of women as celebrated by churches, witch-hunters, and other sexists.* Philadelphia: Westminster, 1973. 190 p.

A general history of sexism in Western civilization. For many centuries the psychological concept of projection was unknown, so that men believed that expressions of female sexuality and allurement were attributable to the woman exercising magical powers over her admirer. Thus the Church's longstanding fear of women's sexuality became a major factor in the witch-hunts. Van Vuuren also writes that unappealing characteristics of women in sexist society, such as deviousness and neuroticism, are due to centuries of discrimination and are common among oppressed peoples.

**671.** Véquaud, Yves. *Women painters of Mithila.* London: Thames and Hudson, 1977. 112 p.

For 3000 years the women of this matrifocal culture in northeast India have been creating intricate religious paintings of Hindu deities and motifs. This highly symbolic art is created exclusively by women. The themes often deal with marriage, but in its spiritual as well as human sense. The illustrations are by thirty women of the Mithila community.

672. Vermaseren, Maarten. *Cybele and Attis: the myth and the cult.* London: Thames and Hudson, 1977. 224 p.

On Cybele's origins as the Great Goddess in Asia Minor and Crete, her worship in Rome and the provinces, and the struggle of her cult with Christianity in the last days of the Roman Empire. Many illustrations.

673. Verryn, Trevor. "The mother archetype," *Theologia Evangelica,* 15(3):49-63, Dec. 1982.

Using examples from Hinduism, the author writes of the Mother as the source of all life whose dark side is She Who Consumes.

674. Vidman, Ladislav. *Isis und Sarapis bei den Griechen und Romern: epigraphische Studien zur Verbreitung und zu den Trägern des ägyptischen Kultes [Isis and Sarapis among the Greeks and Romans: epigraphical studies on the spread and transmission of the Egyptian cult].* Berlin: De Gruyter, 1970. 189 p.

Scholarly study of the worship of Isis and her consort Sarapis, its relationship to other Near Eastern Goddess cults, and its decline in the fourth century.

675. Voegelin, Charles F. *The Shawnee female deity.* New Haven: Yale University Press, 1936. (Yale University Publications in Anthropology, no. 10) 21 p.

On the Shawnee Creator-Goddess known as Our Grandmother.

676. Vogh, James. *Arachne rising: the search for the thirteenth sign of the zodiac.* New York: Dial, 1977. 242 p.

Vogh writes that there should be thirteen signs of the zodiac, not twelve. The missing sign is Arachne, the Spider Woman, now known as the constellation Auriga, which is situated between Taurus and Gemini.

677. Von Bothmer, Dietrich. *Amazons in Greek art.* Oxford: Clarendon Press, 1957. 252 p., 90 plates.

An exhaustive catalogue of Amazons as depicted in Greek statuary and pottery. Includes many illustrations and a list of collections of Amazon art.

678. *Vorträge über Gestalt und Kult der "Grossen Mutter" [Lectures on the image and cult of the Great Mother],* ed. Olga Frobe-

Kapteyn. Zurich: Rhein-Verlag, 1939 (Eranos Jahrbuch, v. 6). 491 p.

Essays, all in German, on the worship of the Great Mother in Anatolia, Crete, the Near East, Islam, India, and the Celtic Realms, and as the Virgin Mary and Jungian archetype. Contributors include Vera Collum (see item 130).

**679.** Waite, Arthur E. *A pictorial key to the Tarot: being fragments of a secret tradition under the veil of divination.* Illus. by Pamela Colman Smith. New York: Harper and Row, 1980; originally published in London, 1910. 340 p.

The Smith-Waite deck, drawn by Smith under the direction of Waite, has been one of the most important Tarot decks in use until the appearance of the new feminist decks, and is still widely used by feminists. (Gearhart and Rennie have pointed out that most of the ostensibly male figures in the cards actually have an androgynous appearance.) The design and interpretations of the cards are based in part upon the Rosicrucian-oriented philosophy of the Hermetic Order of the Golden Dawn, an occult circle that flourished in the late nineteenth and early twentieth centuries. Its members included Smith and Waite, William Butler Yeats, S. L. MacGregor Mathers, and Aleister Crowley. There is an occult tradition that the Tarot originated in ancient times, no later than Egyptian, but Waite did not agree with this. One of the most important contributions made by Smith and Waite is that each card in the four Minor Arcana suits has been given an individual illustration related to its divinitory meaning, making the entire deck more accessible to the unconscious. Includes an annotated bibliography.

**680.** Wakayama, Mary. "Goddesses," *Ka Huliau* (Honolulu), 1(1):17, Nov. 1982.

A review of Mayumi Oda's exhibit of serigraph Goddess images (see entry 494).

**681.** Walker, Barbara G. *The secrets of the Tarot: origins, history, and symbolism.* San Francisco: Harper and Row, 1984. 260 p.

Walker stresses the Goddess-oriented origins of the Tarot and reminds us that playing cards—a truncated version of the ancient Tarot—have long been denounced by churchmen who have been consciously or unconsciously aware of the cards' secret religious symbolism. Her work is illustrated by her own unusual, colorful Tarot deck along with an extensive interpretation for each card and its mythological foundations. The images are reminiscent of those created by Smith and Waite (see above) but are darker and more ominous.

**682.** ———. *The woman's encyclopedia of myths and secrets.* New York: Harper and Row, 1983. 1124 p.

A comprehensive one-volume encyclopedia of the mythology, folklore, history, and symbolism of Goddess religion, magic, and witchcraft. Walker explains that few reference works on mythology or religion have acknowledged the ancient supremacy of the Mother Goddess, let alone traced surviving myths, religious symbols, and folk customs to the pre-patriarchal worship of the Goddess. In her encyclopedia, which covers such topics as cats, chakras, prostitution, sacred mountains, Mary Magdalene, and the odor of sancitity, the author uncovers many features of Goddess religion and pre-Christian paganism. This work would be especially useful for studying the survival of pagan elements within Christianity.

**683.** Walker, Mitch, and friends. *Visionary love: a spirit book of gay mythology and trans-mutational Faerie.* San Francisco: Treeroots Press, 1980. 102 p.

The friends include a woman, H. Constance. This is a gay men's counterpart to feminist spirituality, which is the source of its inspiration. Walker's intention is to explore gayness as shamanism and as a bridge between the male and female principles. His work contains meditations and a great deal of his personal mythology.

**684.** Warner, Marina. *Alone of all her sex: the myth and cult of the Virgin Mary.* New York: Knopf, 1976. 419 p.

The Virgin from a post-feminist perspective. Warner, who was devoted to Mary as a child, has studied Mary in her five major aspects—Virgin, Queen, Bride, Mother, and Intercessor—tracing the evolution of Mariology from the few pertinent Biblical passages to the mediaeval veneration of her as a quasi-goddess. She pays special attention to the development of church theology and to Mary's iconography. Warner also calls attention to the pagan elements of Mary's cult, particularly in her relationship to the Virgin Goddess, the moon, and the serpent.

**685.** Waschnitius, Viktor. *Perht, Holda und verwandte Gestalten: ein Beitrag zur deutschen Religionsgeschicht [Perht, Holda, and related figures: a contribution to German religious history].* Vienna: Alfred Holder, 1913. (Sitzungberichte der Akademie der Wissenschaft, Vienna. Philosophisch-historische Klasse, v. 174, pt. 2) 184 p.

Perht and Holda are Germanic forms of the Earth Goddess, appearing throughout German-speaking areas of Europe and in Scandinavia. Perht is often depicted as the night demon who steals children, while Holda is more closely related to the classic Mother Goddess who appears in Grimm's fairy tales as Mother Holda, the old woman connected with housework.

686. Washbourn, Penelope. *Becoming woman: the quest for wholeness in female experience.* New York: Harper and Row, 1977. 174 p.

Washbourn illustrates how the biological and social experiences of womanhood reveal profound truths about identity, spirituality, and personal growth. In so doing she teaches us that within the female experience the line between psychology and spirituality is very fine.

687. ――――, ed. *Seasons of woman: song, poetry, ritual, prayer, myth, story.* San Francisco: Harper and Row, 1979. 176 p.

A collection of creative literature from women of many cultures, both ancient and contemporary, including African, Native American, and Polynesian, that celebrates the stages of a woman's life, from childhood to puberty to motherhood to old age.

688. Wasson, R. Gordon, Albert Hofmann, and Carl A. A. Ruck. *The road to Eleusis: unveiling the secret of the Mysteries.* New York: Harcourt, Brace, Jovanovich, 1977. 124 p.

On the use of hallucinogenic drugs in the Eleusinian Mysteries. Wasson, a highly respected ethnobotanist and mycologist who has written on the soma of India and on Mexican magic mushrooms, believes that the fragmentary and veiled descriptions of the Mysteries suggest that the hallucinogenic mushroom known as the fly agaric was used as a sacrament in the course of an initiation. This book includes the text of the "Homeric Hymn to Demeter," which is the chief source of information on the sacred rites, and many photographs of artifacts used in the rituals.

689. Webster, Paula. "Matriarchy: a vision of power," in *Toward an Anthropology of Women,* ed. Rayna R. Reiter. New York: Monthly Review Press, 1975, p. 141-56.

A revised version of a paper she wrote with Esther Newton (see entry 478). She concludes that the *reality* of female supremacy may be so hard to document that it implies historical non-existence, but points out that the *vision* of matriarchy forces us to question social and political assumptions. "Though the matriarchy debate revolves around the past, its real value lies in the future... It pushes women (and men) to imagine a society that is not patriarchal, one in which women might for the first time have power over their lives."

690. Wedeck, Harry. *A treasury of witchcraft.* New York: Philosophical Library, 1961. 271 p.

A compendium of spells, incantations, and general witch lore taken from many old documents and ancient writings. The selections tend to be oriented toward black magic, but there is quite a bit of authentic material collected in this book.

691. Weenolsen, Hebe. *The forbidden mountain.* New York: William Morrow, 1983. 353 p.

A novel on the construction of Stonehenge III (the main structure visible today), in the second millenium B.C. The story centers on the conflict between the indigenous Goddess-worshipping people and the ruling tribe of sun-worshipping Beaker Folk, who modified Stonehenge to reflect a solar, rather than a lunar, cosmology.

692. Weigle, Martha. *Spiders and spinsters: women and mythology.* Albuquerque: University of New Mexico Press, 1982. 340 p.

A imaginative, well-researched book on women in fairy tales and Classical and Native American mythology. Each chapter contains selections from mythographers such as Neumann and Graves and the texts of Native American and Classical myths. An excellent resource for the study of women in Native American mythology.

693. Weinstein, Marion. *Earth magic: a Dianic Book of Shadows;* with illustrations by the author. Custer, WA: Phoenix Publishing Co., in cooperation with Earth Magic Productions, New York City, 1980. 48 p.

A useful manual that includes information not often found elsewhere, e.g. on familiars and spells. Weinstein describes the Craft concept of magic and power, the use of candles and ritual tools, the coven structure, and lunar and seasonal rites.

694. ———. *Positive magic: occult self-help.* Rev. ed. Custer, WA: Phoenix Publishing Co., 1981. 283 p.

A down-to-earth introduction to the occult that gives sensible advice for the novice on occult skills and what to look (out) for when joining groups. Explains the uses of astrology, Tarot cards, the *I Ching,* and the occult philosophy in general. There is also an extensive section on the use of Words of Power, i.e. affirmations and creative meditation.

695. ———. "The witch-myth: take my broom... please," *Majority Report,* 8(12):9, Oct. 14, 1978.

On a witch's experiences with the media, and on the media's representation of the Craft.

696. *We'moon Almanac: an astrological moon calendar for [women]; a daily guide to natural rhythms.* Edited by Musawa. La Scrrc Darrc, Pouzac 65200, France; distributed by *WomanSpirit,* Wolf Creek, OR 97497-9799.

An annual lunar calendar and datebook with daily information on the planets and short articles on astrology, healing, and moon lore, primarily from the Scandinavian and Celtic traditions. Contributions by Monica Sjöö and others.

**697.** Werz-Kovacs, Stephanie von. *"Heilige Mutterschaft": Rekonstruktion matriarchalischer Elemente in der Religion und Mythologie der altindischen Bhil ["Holy motherhood": a reconstruction of the matriarchal elements in the religion and mythology of the Old-Indian Bhil].* Munich: Minerva Publikation, 1982. 302 p.

Based on the author's doctoral dissertation (with title: *Rekonstruktion matriarchalischer Elemente...*) on the Bhil people of India.

**698.** Wesel, Uwe. *Der Mythos vom Matriarchat: über Bachofens Mutterrecht und der Stellung von Frauen in frühen Gesellschaften vor den Entstehung staatliche Herrschaft [The myth of matriarchy: on Bachofen's "Mother-Right" and the position of women in early society before the origin of political power].* Frankfurt am Main: Suhrkamp, 1980. 167 p.

**699.** Wheat, Valerie. "The return of the Goddess," *Booklegger Magazine,* 2(7):10–17, Jan. 1975.

A survey of the women's spirituality movement with an extensive annotated bibliography of relevant books and periodicals published through 1974.

**700.** Whitmont, Edward C. *The return of the Goddess.* New York: Crossroad, 1982. 272 p.

On the psychology of aggression and the desperate need for the return of the feminine principle. Whitmont believes that the domination of the unconscious, of which the witch-hunts are the most striking example, was a necessary development in humanity's struggle towards self-awareness.

**701.** "Wicca goes to court," *Sister,* 9(1):2, Feb. 1978.

**702.** *Wicce: A lesbian/feminist newspaper.* Philadelphia, 1973–.

**703.** Willard, Nancy. "Goddess in the belfry," *Parabola,* 6(3):90–94, Summer 1981.

On the Goddess and the Old Wise Woman as they appear in George MacDonald's Victorian fairy tales. In many of MacDonald's stories the Divine is represented by a feminine figure, often elderly, who has her dark side as well as beneficent characteristics.

**704.** Williams, Selma R., and Pamela J. Williams. *Riding the nightmare: women and witchcraft.* New York: Atheneum, 1978. 228 p.

The authors—mother and daughter—use trial records to show that convicted and executed witches were twenty times as likely to be women as men, and that this phenomenon was motivated by misogyny and the pursuit of total male domination in society. Most of the book deals with the European witch-hunts but the authors also consider witchcraft in ancient civilizations.

705. Winant, Fran. *Dyke jacket: poems and songs.* New York: Violet Press, 1976. 63 p.

Includes some early poems about the Goddess. Winant provides the reader with one of the best comebacks to the Christian sidewalk evangelist: "Oh, I belong to the Religion of the Goddess." Confuses the hell out of them.

706. ———. *The Goddess of lesbian dreams: poems and songs.* New York: Violet Press, 1980. 64 p.

707. ———. "When God was a woman," *Women,* 6(1):58, 1978.

708. Winter, Urs. *Frau und Göttin: exegetische und ikonographische Studien zum weiblichen Gottesbild im alten Israel und dessen Umwelt [Woman and Goddess: exegetical and iconographic studies on the feminine imagery of God in Ancient Israel and the surrounding lands].* Freiburg, Switzerland: Unversitätsverlag; Göttingen, Germany: Vandenhoeck and Ruprecht, 1983 (PhD thesis, University of Freiburg). 748 p., 178 p. of plates.

A monumental work on goddesses of the Near East, women in the Bible, the image of woman in Genesis and the masculinity of Jehovah, and women among the Hebrews and in the non-Judaic Near East. Includes a fifty-page bibliography on Near Eastern religion.

709. *The Wise Woman.* Temple of the Goddess Within, 2442 Cordova St., Oakland CA 94602, 1980-.

Quarterly periodical oriented toward Feminist Wicca and Goddess religion, edited by Ann Forfreedom.

710. "WITCH documents," in *Sisterhood is powerful: an anthology of writings from the women's liberation movement,* ed. Robin Morgan. New York: Random House, 1970, p. 539-46; New York: Vintage Books, 1970, p. 603-21.

A collection of articles, pamphlets, and poetry by the members of the Women's International Terrorist Conspiracy from Hell, the first feminist organization to recognise the connection between witchcraft and the fight against women's oppression. One of the documents is the historic WITCH Manifesto, proclaiming that "you are a Witch by being female, untamed, angry, joyous, and immortal."

**711.** "Witchcraft," *Everywoman,* 2(8):4, May 28, 1971.
An article about Anne Steward, a Tucson high school teacher fired for being a witch—a charge that was never substantiated.

**712.** *Witchcraft in Europe and America.* Woodbridge, CT: Research Publications, 1983. 104 microfilm reels.
Contains over 1000 books and manuscripts spanning the 16th through the 20th centuries, mostly from the collections at Cornell University and the University of Pennsylvania.

**713.** *Witchcraft in Europe and America: guide to the microfilm collection, ed. by Diane M. Del Cuervo.* Woodbridge, CT: Research Publications, 1983. 111 p.
See previous entry.

**714.** Witches International Craft Associates. *WICA Newsletter.* 153 W. 80th St., New York, NY 10024: Hero Press.
Newsletter published by Leo Martello, one of the leaders of the early Neo-Pagan movement in America, who has long supported the equality of women in the Craft.

**715.** Witt, Reginald E. *Isis in the Graeco-Roman world.* Ithaca, NY: Cornell University Press, 1971. 336 p.
A comprehensive study of Isis. Begins with Isis as a purely Egyptian deity and traces the spread and survival of her worship into late Classical times. Witt describes Isis as the Great Mother of Life and discusses her connections with goddesses such as Artemis. Many illustrations.

**716.** Wittig, Monique. *Les Guérillères.* New York: Viking Press, 1971; New York: Avon, 1973. 144 p.
An epic prose-poem—*the* epic—of women's liberation. Startlingly contemporary in its politics and understanding of women's mythic history, considering that it was written in 1968, at the dawn of the modern feminist movement. Wittig's vision and creative use of language continue to have a powerful effect upon feminist thought and literature. In her story of women together, Wittig alludes to several historical stages: a Golden Age of sisterly harmony, an age of technology and historical consciousness, a military struggle against patriarchy, and a reconciliation between the women and the young men who have fought on their side. At intervals in the text she lists hundreds of women's given names from many different cultures, creating both a feminine liturgy and a timeless myth. It is from *Les Guérillères* that the motto of matriarchal feminism is taken: "There was a time when you were not a slave, remember that. You walked alone, full of laughter, you bathed bare-bellied. You say you have lost all

recollection of it, remember... You say there are no words to describe this time, you say it does not exist. But remember. Make an effort to remember. Or, failing that, invent."

**717.** ———. *The lesbian body.* New York: William Morrow, 1976; Avon, 1976. 159 p.

Wittig again creates an exclusively female world, in which she celebrates the love for women's bodies with violent passion. Here the list of women's names has been replaced by lists of body parts. There are also several hymns of praise to Sappho and to the Goddess.

**718.** Wittig, Monique, and Sande Zeig. *Lesbian peoples: material for a dictionary.* New York: Avon, 1979. 170 p.

Perhaps this work can best be described as a visionary dictionary written in a lesbian-feminist world in which a vanishing powder has made everyone but lesbians disappear. Many of the entries deal with Amazon lore; some are politically instructive ("Woman" is defined as "slave"—we are now known as "companion-lovers"), while others are fanciful: in the entry for "Fur" we read, "Numerous companion-lovers have adopted fur implants of all kinds on their skin..." Here Wittig continues her work of creating an exclusively lesbian language and literature.

**719.** Wolf, Eric. "The Virgin of Guadalupe: a Mexican national symbol," *Journal of American Folklore*, 71:34-39, 1958.

On the Virgin's Goddess origins and the meaning she has had for Mexicans, particularly those of Native heritage.

**720.** Wolkstein, Diane, and Samuel N. Kramer. *Inanna, queen of heaven and earth: her stories and hymns from Sumer.* San Francisco: Harper and Row, 1983. 227 p.

A compilation of the ancient myths featuring Inanna, rearranged to make a coherent story of her descent to Ereshkigal, the Dark Queen of the Underworld (her sister and other self). Illustrated with ancient sculpture and cuneiform tablets which are interpreted by art historian Elizabeth Williams Forte. Samuel Kramer, who is considered the leading authority on Sumerian culture and religion, gives Inanna's genealogy and background to the texts, while Wolkstein, a professional storyteller, provides interpretations of the myths.

**721.** *Woman of Power.* Box 827, Cambridge, MA 02238-0827. Spring 1984-.

A new periodical concentrating on feminism, spirituality and politics. As of 1986 three issues have appeared. Each issue focuses on a particular theme; future topics include women of color, healing, and international feminism. The magazine is handsomely produced and contains articles by Susan Griffin, Starhawk, Diane Mariechild, Charlene Spretnak, Dhyani Ywahoo, and many other women involved in spirituality and feminist political action.

722. *WomanSpirit.* Wolf Creek, OR, 1974–84. Quarterly.

The first and most important magazine of feminist spirituality. Published almost singlehandedly by Jean and Ruth Mountaingrove on a miniscule budget, this has been an important resource for articles, poetry, rituals, book reviews, news of gatherings of women, and the many issues of feminism over the past decade. Jean and Ruth consciously intended the magazine to be a forum for any woman with something of value to say to women, and their editorial acceptance of an array of writing styles and philosophies made *WomanSpirit* truly reflective of the grass roots of the feminist spirituality movement. In addition to contributions by many first-time authors, relevant articles were often reprinted from other feminist and progressive periodicals. Most of the feminist authors in this bibliography have appeared in *WomanSpirit.* It is greatly missed.

723. Womantree, Kim. "Hexes to holy wars: nonpolitical 'pure' spirituality has never existed," *Big Mama Rag*, 10(3):14–15, March 1982.

The author states quite firmly that all forms of spirituality are political, whether they support oppression or are revolutionary. Women's spirituality can be a progressive force if it strengthens the group and has a commitment to concrete political action.

724. *Women and religion: a bibliography selected from the ATLA Religion Database.* 3rd rev. ed. Chicago: American Theological Library Association Religion Indexes, 1983. 660 p.

Concentrates on women in traditional religion.

725. *Women's Coven Newsletter.* 5756 Vicente St., Oakland CA 94609.

A now-defunct periodical for women in feminist witchcraft.

726. Worth, Valerie. *The crone's book of words.* St. Paul: Llewellyn Publications, 1971. 155 p.

Spells and charms in verse, many describing herbal remedies.

727. Wright, Thomas, ed. *A contemporary narrative of the proceedings against Dame Alice Kyteler: prosecuted for sorcery in 1324 by Richard de Ledrede, Bishop of Ossory.* London: Camden Society, 1843. (Camden Society Publications, no. 24) 140 p.

Alice Kyteler, an Irish noblewoman, was one of the earliest women to be prosecuted in the great witch-hunts. Apparently the charges were initiated by family members hoping to gain control of her lands. She was acquitted, but her servants, including a woman named Petronilla, were burned. The proceedings of her trial are in Latin, taken from Harleian MS 641. An English introduction gives the background to witchcraft practices and their penalties in England and Ireland, and contains the Latin texts of some government pronouncements on witchcraft. Notes to the Proceedings are appended (in English).

**728.** Xarai, Max. *Witch dream: matriarchal comix.* Oakland, CA: The Women's Press Collective; distributed by the Crossing Press, Trumansburg, NY, 1974. 37 p.

Two stories in comic-strip form: "Witch Dream," in which a visit to a museum sends a woman psychically back to matriarchal times, where she grows up under the tutelage of the tribal wise woman, and "The Rise of the Amazing Amazons," a mythic history of the war against patriarchy.

**729.** Yates, Gayle Graham. "Spirituality and the American feminist experience," *Signs,* 9(1):59-72, Autumn 1983.

This issue has a special section on women and religion. Yates gives an overview of the work of feminist thinkers such as Daly, Christ, and Ochs, and discusses selected historical studies, religious works on the Goddess, and spirituality in the writings of Annie Dillard and Alice Walker.

**730.** Zabriskie, Philip. "Goddesses in our midst," *Quadrant* (New York: C. G. Jung Foundation), no. 17 (Fall, 1974), p. 34–45.

On the psychological power of the ancient feminine archetypes still to be found in Classical goddesses.

**731.** Zahler, Leah. "Matriarchy and myth," *Aphra,* 4(3):25-31, Summer 1973.

An overview of the concept of matriarchy and matrifocal, Goddess-centered culture as described by Jane Ellen Harrison, Robert Graves, Joseph Campbell, and Erich Neumann. Zahler concludes that what is important for women today is not matriarchy as historical fact but matriarchy as a model for women's community.

**732.** Zana. *Herb womon.* 2000 King Mountain Trail, Sunny Valley, OR 97497: New Woman Press, 1984.

Poetry and art by a disabled lesbian witch who was a frequent contributor to *WomanSpirit.*

**733.** Zell, Morning Glory. "Magick words: witchcraft," *Eugene Augur,* 3(1):7, Sept. 17, 1971.

Her first column on the Craft; explains her background, witchcraft, and the Goddess and God. Morning Glory is a priestess in the Church of All Worlds, a new Pagan religion based on witchcraft and on Robert Heinlein's philosophy in *Stranger in a Strange Land* (see Margot Adler, *Drawing Down the Moon*).

734. ———. "Magick words: the festival of death," *Eugene Augur*, 3(4):6, Nov. 5, 1971.
On Halloween and its Celtic originators.

735. ———. "Magick words: the White Goddess and her children," *Eugene Augur*, 3(5):6, Nov. 19, 1971.
On the Goddess and witchcraft, and the patriarchal oppression of women.

736. Zimmer, Heinrich R. *Die indische Weltmutter [The Indian World-Mother]*. Frankfurt am Main: Insel-Verlag, 1980 (Eranos Jahrbuch, v. 6, 1939). 253 p.

737. Zinser, Hartmut. *Der Mythos der Mutterrechts: Verhandlung von drei aktuellen Theorien des Geschlechter Kampfes [The myth of motheright: a treatment of three contemporary theories of the war between the sexes]*. Frankfurt am Main: Ullstein, 1981. 96 p.
Emphasizes the religious aspects of the mythology of matriarchy and its relationship to sex roles.

738. Zografou, Mina. *Amazons in Homer and Hesiod (a historical reconstruction)*. Athens, 1972. 165 p.
In the *Iliad* Homer describes the Amazons, led by Queen Penthesilea, as battling the Greeks on the side of the Trojans. The works of Homer and Hesiod (see item 305), whose writings date from the eighth century B.C., are among the earliest literature of the Greeks and are often used by historians as a window into the Indo-European heroic age. Some historians have interpreted the Trojan War as a mythic retelling of the Bronze Age incursions of Indo-European patriarchal peoples.

739. Zuntz, Gunther. *Persephone: three essays on religion and thought in Magna Graecia*. Oxford: Clarendon Press, 1971. 427 p.
The relevant essay is the first, on Persephone as "The Goddess of Sicily." Magna Graecia was the name for the Greek colony on Sicily. A Mother Goddess had been worshipped there by the indigenous Italic people, but after the Greeks colonized the island the primordial goddess was transmuted into Persephone. She was thereafter worshipped more often in her aspect of goddess of the Underworld and death than as daughter of Demeter.

# SUBJECT INDEX

Africa, 12, 62, 156, 235, 268, 294, 396, 477, 499, 592, 644, 651, 687
Amazons, 1, 2, 52, 62, 156, 171, 179, 191, 218, 307, 337, 441, 450, 500, 550, 581, 595, 596, 597, 630, 664, 677, 718, 728, 738
American Indians—*see* Native Americans, Latin America
Anath, 73, 108, 189, 317, 338
Anatolia, 44, 217, 274, 301, 323, 371, 436, 672, 678; *see also* Çatal Hüyük
Anthropology, 38, 42, 344, 345, 478, 504, 574, 657, 689
Aphrodite, 236, 243, 280, 354, 648
Archaeology, 44, 160, 161, 256, 295, 335, 436, 509
Ariadne, 79, 532, 555
Art, 14, 16, 54, 59, 115, 116, 117, 132, 140, 162, 194, 195, 204, 215, 217, 252, 261, 264, 301, 329, 351, 359, 376, 382, 383, 384, 404, 494, 541, 550, 592, 613, 625, 629, 644, 661, 671, 677, 680, 696, 720, 721, 722, 728, 732
Artemis, 52, 217
Arthurian legend, 74, 226
Asia Minor—*see* Anatolia
Asian women, 14, 341, 636; *see also* China, Japan, Pacific peoples, Buddhism, *etc.*
Astarte, 317
Astrology, 37, 68, 310, 511, 515, 656, 676, 696
Athena, 7, 244, 352
Australia, 56, 592, 644
Babylon, 379, 390
Basques, 314, 502, 503
Bible, 150, 193, 215, 375, 401, 448, 449, 492, 513, 529, 590, 652, 708
Bibliographies, 119, 135, 205, 214, 215, 270, 272, 438, 523, 559, 561, 699, 708, 724
Birth, 14, 54, 115, 197, 341, 491, 686, 687
Black women, 12, 47, 62, 109, 218, 294, 396, 438, 483, 559, 609, 636, 651; *see also* Africa, Brazil
Bona Dea, 509, 524

## ABOUT THE AUTHOR

Anne Carson grew up in Tenafly, New Jersey and attended Carnegie-Mellon University, where she received a bachelor's degree in history and English. She went on to do graduate research on women in early Christian Ireland, earning master's degrees in mediaeval history and library science at the University of Pittsburgh. She also received a black belt in karate while in Pittsburgh, and began to study feminist spirituality. Her first published works appeared in *WomanSpirit* magazine. She catalogued rare books at Brown University before moving to Ithaca, New York, where she lives with her husband David and her cat Thuvia. She works as a librarian at Cornell University, and in her spare time she grows herbs and watches the moon.